# COMPANIONS

## QUILTS AND MINIATURES

by
**Darlene Zimmerman**

EZ International
95 Mayhill Street
Saddle Brook, NJ 07662

## Acknowledgements

I'm forever grateful to my husband, Don, and my children for giving me the time and freedom to pursue my obsession with quilting.

Special thanks go to:

The Aufderheide family for lending the antique quilts pictured in this book.

Jo and Ormon Wilson for all their help and encouragement.

Joy Hoffman and Theresa Westrup for pattern testing and their wonderful quilting.

Lynette Jensen for her helpful advice.

Sharon Hultgren and Chuck Sabosik at EZ for believing in me.

Mimi and John Shimp at SPPS for putting it all together.

And all the others who helped along the way.

Published in the United States by EZ International, 95 Mayhill Street, Saddle Brook, NJ 07662. Printed in Hong Kong

ISBN: 1-881588-00-9.

To the memory of my mentor and friend

Joyce Aufderheide

who introduced me to the
wonderful world of quilt-making,
and made all of this possible.

# *Preface*

This book is not intended as a complete guide to quilt-making. There are many wonderful books on the market today that give complete and in-depth information. I suggest you visit your local quilt shop for help in this area. I am simply sharing with you some of the ideas or techniques I've learned from personal experience – usually the hard way. My philosophy is that there are no hard and fast rules for quilt-making. Feel free to use whatever techniques or methods with which you feel most comfortable to get the job done!

Whenever you are in doubt about what size to cut when you are using a pattern or block not included in this book, simply lay the tool over the template, and add on seam allowances.

There is a tutorial section explaining the use of the tools used in this book. Please review it carefully if you are not familiar with the tools. The correct sizes to cut for the projects are listed with the individual projects.

Read over the directions in all the instructional sections before beginning any project, particularly miniatures. The tips given may help to eliminate potential problems. Finally, there is a section on finishing and a half-block chart at the end of the book to take the figuring out of your hands!

# Table of Contents

# Tool Tutorial
# and
# Basic Construction Techniques

# *Using Companion Angle*™

Use Companion Angle™ to make triangles with the long edge on the outside of a block, border, or quilt. Cut the triangles with the long edge on the straight of the grain to prevent distortion.

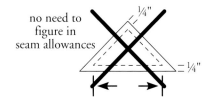

Dashed lines represent sewing lines and show the **finished** triangle size, based on a ¼" seam allowance; center numbers represent the width of the strip to cut; solid lines underneath are used for alignment (for example, cut a 2½" strip for **finished** 4" triangles.)

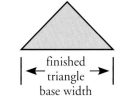

Determine the required size of the long edge of your finished triangle.

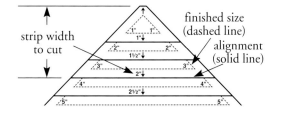

Determine the required strip width to cut to get the desired triangle size.

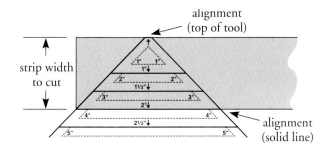

Align the tool edge with the edge of the strip.

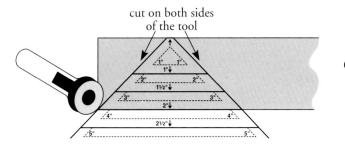

Cut on both sides of the tool.

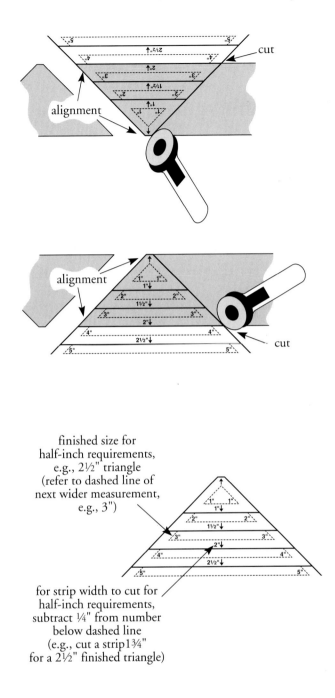

Invert the tool and cut another triangle; continue in this manner across the strip of fabric.

As you continue across the strip, make sure that the top of the tool, the alignment line you are using, and the edge of the triangle are positioned correctly.

finished size for half-inch requirements, e.g., 2½" triangle (refer to dashed line of next wider measurement, e.g., 3")

for strip width to cut for half-inch requirements, subtract ¼" from number below dashed line (e.g., cut a strip 1¾" for a 2½" finished triangle)

You can use this tool to cut triangles that have other than whole inch long edges. The role of the dashed and solid lines are reversed. Align on dashed line.

# *Trapezoids*

To cut any trapezoid with Companion Angle™, you need to measure the finished width of the base and the finished height. Add ½" to the height (two ¼" seam allowances to get the strip width.)

On the tool, find the dashed line for the desired finished base width. The solid line directly beneath will be the line on which to align your fabric.

Align the fabric strip to the line so it extends on both sides of the tool. Cut on both sides of the tool.

Invert the tool and align the top of the strip with the solid line and the cut edge of the fabric. Cut on the right.

The alignment line on Companion Angle™ for trapezoids will be the line under the line representing the required finished base width. If the finished width is a whole number of inches (e.g., 6"), use the solid line underneath the appropriate dashed line. If it includes a half-inch (e.g., 5½") use the next higher (e.g., 6") dashed line for alignment.

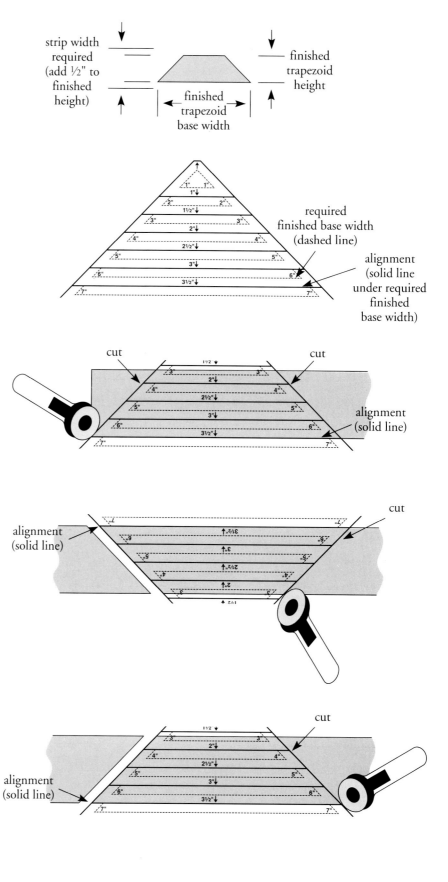

# Using Easy Angle™

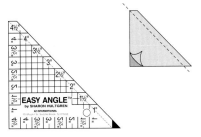

Easy Angle™ provides a quick method to cut right triangles. Just add seam allowance to your finished size, place two cut strips of fabric right sides together, then counter-cut with the Easy Angle™. The lines on the tool are provided at ¼" increments, and are used for aligning fabric strips for cutting. The heavier lines are provided at ½" increments.

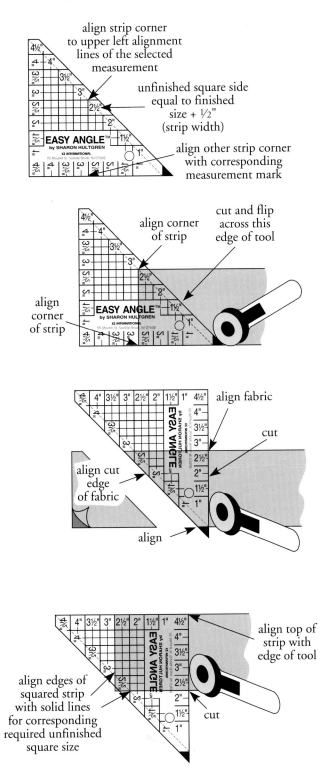

align strip corner to upper left alignment lines of the selected measurement

unfinished square side equal to finished size + ½" (strip width)

align other strip corner with corresponding measurement mark

cut and flip across this edge of tool

align corner of strip

align corner of strip

align fabric

cut

align cut edge of fabric

align

align top of strip with edge of tool

align edges of squared strip with solid lines for corresponding required unfinished square size

cut

Use of the tool requires that you select a finished square size. Once you do this, add ½" to get the corresponding unfinished triangle size. Find the unfinished size on the tool and the alignment lines above and to the left of this number.

Cut strips equal to the unfinished width of the triangle size. Lay the strips right sides together. Align the bottom of the tool on the bottom edge of the strip. Slide the tool to the right until the end of the strip aligns with the strip width number at the bottom. Cut along the long edge of the tool.

Flip the tool over the long edge and align the tool so that the cut edge of the fabric aligns with the tool and the bottom edge of the fabric aligns with the top of the black triangle on the tool. Cut along the perpendicular edge of the tool. Repeat these last two steps until you have cut all of your triangles. You will have pairs of triangles which you may string through your machine to make the triangle-squares. Note that the pieces for the square are already right sides together.

To make single fabric squares up to 4½", cut a strip equal to the unfinished square size. Align the tool with the top edge of the strip and slide it along the strip until the left side of the strip aligns with the vertical line on the tool representing the unfinished square size.

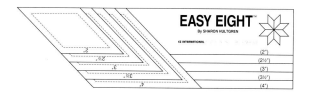

Easy Eight™ makes it easy to do the eight-pointed stars you will find in several of the projects. It allows for five sizes of diamonds, as indicated on the tool.

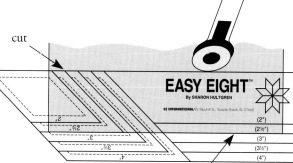

required finished
diamond side length

find finished diamonds
measurement and
line beneath

This tool is very easy to use. First determine the length of the side of your finished diamond. Then find that number on the tool, and the corresponding line underneath. The 2½" size is chosen as an example.

Fold your fabric and square up one end perpendicular to the folds. Lay the tool over the edge and line up the edge with the line underneath the finished diamond size number. Then cut strips. Note that the width of the strip will not be the same as the alignment number on the tool. The number represents the diamond size and the line underneath gives the strip width.

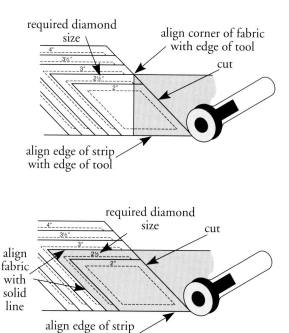

cut

line up squared edge
of folded fabric on line
corresponding to diamond size

When cutting the diamonds from the strip, turn the tool around and line up the strip with the tool as indicated. Cut the triangle off of the corner.

required diamond
size

align corner of fabric
with edge of tool

cut

align edge of strip
with edge of tool

Slide the tool along the strip until the edge of the strip aligns with the solid line representing the outline of the unfinished diamond for the diamond size. Cut the diamond from the strip. Repeat this step for additional diamonds. Repeat these last two steps for each strip.

required diamond
size

cut

align
fabric
with
solid
line

align edge of strip
with edge of tool

# Tool Companions

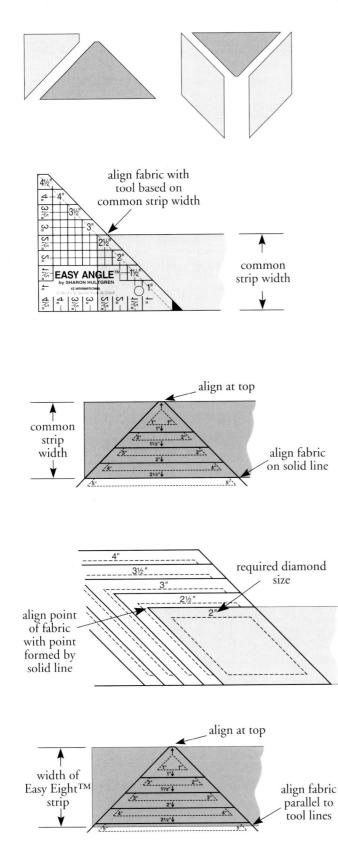

The tools described here are intimately compatible. You will be able to make perfectly matching pieces from Easy Angle™ and Companion Angle™. You will also be able to make exact fitting pieces from Easy Eight™ and Companion Angle™.

Once you select an unfinished square size, cut strips and Easy Angle™ triangles as described earlier. In this instance you will not be cutting these for triangle-squares, so you won't worry about two strips of fabric right sides together.

Cut the same width strips for the matching Companion Angle™ triangles. The strips should line up perfectly with the solid line under the same measurement number you used for cutting strips with Easy Angle™. Cut triangles as described earlier. Flying geese will be a breeze.

Use Easy Eight™ to cut the same width strips for the set-in triangles. Cut the triangles with Companion Angle™.

Align strips at the top of Companion Angle™ and make sure the bottom of the strip is parallel with a line on the tool. The bottom of the strips may not match a line, since the width is entirely dependent on the Easy Eight™ measurements. Just make sure the bottom is parallel.

# Setting In: The Eight Pointed Star

These steps will be used several times in the construction of the Eight Pointed Star. They apply to setting in either a triangle or a square between two diamonds. The diamonds may be completely separate or may be part of another piece. The illustrations below assume piecing a triangle.

First align the triangle point with the point of the diamond right sides together, and stitch. Sew up to ¼" of the adjacent corner of the point and backstitch (for strength.)

Open and press in the direction of the arrow. You will press all of these in the direction indicated in the figure.

Lay this sewn piece right sides together over the second diamond and align as before. Backstitch at the beginning and from the seam allowance at the center to the points.

Press down as before.

Gently fold the piece in half, right sides together, as indicated in the figure. Align the two points of the diamonds. Starting at your previous stitching; stitch to the points.

Open up and press the seam open or to one side. Trim the "dog-ears".

This technique will be used to set in the triangles and squares as shown on the next page. Use it any time two diamonds come together with a set in square or triangle.

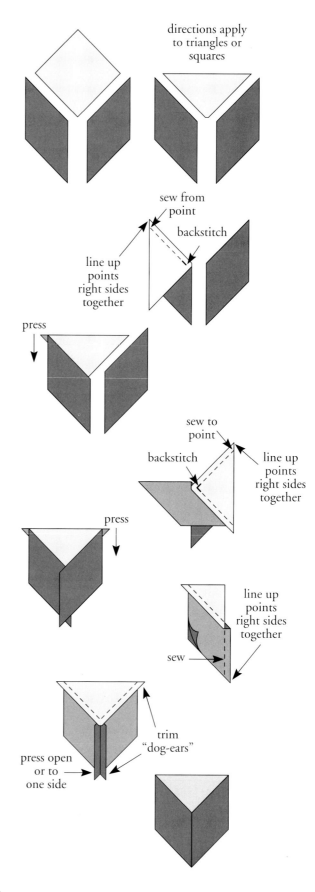

# *Piecing the Eight Pointed Star*

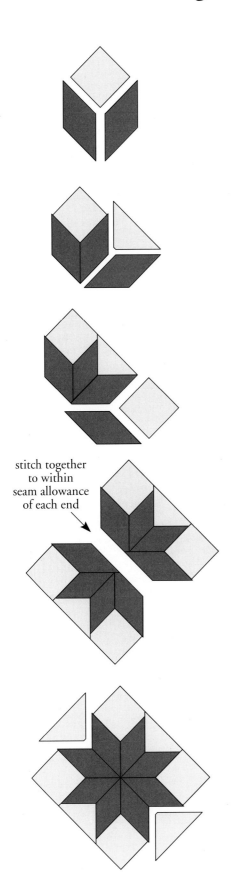

Cut squares ½" larger than the diamond size you have chosen. E.g.: 2" diamond plus ½" equals a 2½" square. Set it into two diamonds using the technique discussed on the previous page.

Set in a triangle between one of the pieced diamonds and another diamond using the same technique.

Set in another square between this piece and another diamond.

stitch together to within seam allowance of each end

Make a second half the same way. Sew these two halves together, matching centers, and making sure that the stitching stops at ¼" from either end of the seam.

Finally, set in the last two triangles. Note that the same setting in technique applies, except that the order of sewing is different. The diamonds have been attached first. Note also that you will need to fold the piece to align the triangle and the last point for sewing.

# *Flying Geese Construction*

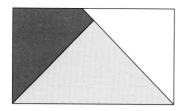

Several of the designs in this collection use the "flying geese" unit, and so the instructions for this technique are detailed here. Refer to this section whenever you need to refresh your memory on "flying geese" construction.

Cut triangles of desired size from Easy Angle™ and Companion Angle™. The strips will be the same width for both types of triangles.

Line up the corners of one Easy Angle™ triangle and one Companion Angle™ triangle and stitch together.

Open and press in the direction of the arrow. Pressing in this direction will emphasize your geese. Pressing in the opposite direction will emphasize the background.

Add the second triangle cut from Easy Angle™ to the Companion Angle™ triangle.

Open and press in the direction of the arrow. Trim the "dog-ears." The point of the goose will be ¼" down from the top edge.

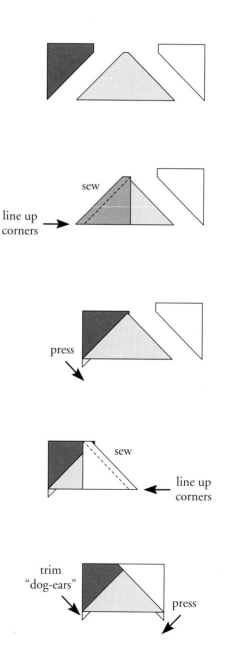

# Design and Construction Tips

### SEWING THE QUARTER INCH SEAM

Sounds simple enough to sew a ¼" seam, doesn't it? Sewing a consistently *accurate* ¼" seam is crucial to quilt-making, and an important skill to master. To find that exact ¼" on *your* sewing machine, place one of your acrylic rulers under your presser foot. Lower the presser foot and line up the needle exactly on the first ¼" marking. Place masking tape on the machine snugly against the edge of your ruler. Use this as an accurate seam guide.

Before sewing, wherever pieces must match up at a seam, line up the seams right sides together, having the seams alternating and pin at each intersection. As you sew the pieces together, it is also helpful to alternate the direction the seams are pressed. This will eliminate some of the bulk you get when several seam allowances come together.

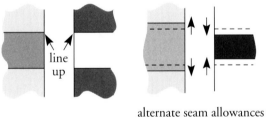

alternate seam allowances
between pieces being
sewn together

As you come to each pin, remove it before sewing over the seam. You don't want your needle to hit one and break, flying off into oblivion!

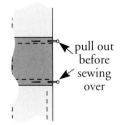

pull out
before
sewing
over

Another technique that should be used whenever possible is chain-sewing. Have the units stacked up next to your sewing machine and simply feed one unit after another through the machine without lifting the presser foot or cutting the thread. This saves time, thread, and helps to eliminate the "gobbling feed dog" problem. After chain-sewing them through, you will need to snip them apart before pressing.

### PRESSING

Small arrows appear in several locations in this book showing pressing directions. If you follow these pressing directions, most, if not all of your seams will alternate. You certainly don't want seam allowances to stack up at an intersection. When I press the pieces I prefer to use a dry iron. Steam is helpful in the final pressing of a quilt top.

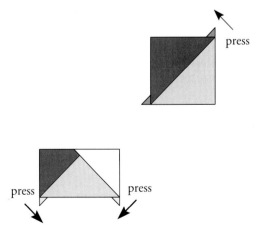

press

press            press

## STACK PRESSING

Stack pressing is a neat, efficient way to press small units such as triangle-squares or flying geese. This is especially helpful when your pieces are tiny. Simply place all units to be pressed by your left hand, dark side up. Lift the corner of the dark triangle, place it on the ironing board, and press the seam towards the dark triangle with the iron in your right hand. Now, pick up the next unit, lay it on top of the first unit pressed, lining up the raw edge of the seam to the previous seam, and press again. Continue in this manner until the stack becomes too thick. (Reverse the procedure if you are left-handed.) This method is not only efficient, but prevents your units from being pressed out of shape.

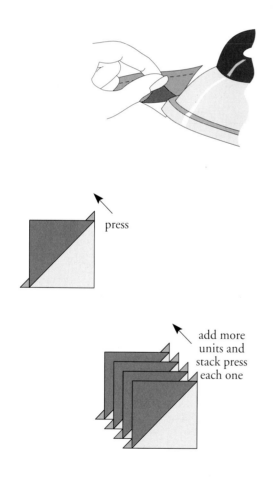

press

add more units and stack press each one

## FABRIC SELECTION AND COLOR CHOICES

Learning color theory and studying the color wheel is helpful, but that doesn't tell you what you like. If you're uncomfortable with choosing fabrics for a quilt, spend some time with quilt books or art picture books and find out which color combinations appeal most to you *before* you shop for fabric. Do you like soft, muted pastels or bright bold prints? When you see a quilt or picture you like, stop and analyze why you like it – is it the color combinations, the contrasts, or the pattern? Think about how you could use these colors in your quilt.

Most of the patterns in the book have a limited number of fabrics. Start by choosing one fabric you really like. Then add more fabrics that either complement or accent the first fabric. Think in terms of texture also – it's more interesting to have a mixture of small and large prints. Stack the bolts and step back ten feet for a better look. Looking at fabric combinations within inches rather than feet can be very deceptive. Colors and patterns that may seem "off" very close, may actually blend and complement each other when viewed from ten feet. From what perspective will the finished quilt be seen? Up close as in a miniature, or back several feet, hanging on a wall or draped on a bed? Consider the fabrics in the same perspective. Keep experimenting until you find a pleasing combination.

One tip to remember is to always include one dark color somewhere in your quilt as an accent. Don't be afraid to use black. Remember in grade school when you colored pictures and then outlined the shapes with a black crayon? You can use black as an accent color just as effectively in a quilt.

A final recommendation – I use only 100% cotton fabrics and pre-wash and iron all of them before use.

# Full Size Projects

# Right and Left
## *66" x 78"*

*See photo on page 33.*

*Right and Left* is an interesting pattern not often used today. When you first look at the quilt you see pinwheels set on point between plain blocks. Look again, and the center square set on point becomes the center of a paddle-wheel block. You can bring out either aspect of the design just with your color placement.

The directions given here indicate four fabrics. As a point of reference, refer to the photograph of the antique *Right and Left* quilt on page 33. The directions associate the four fabrics with those in this quilt. The directions here give requirements for two sizes of this quilt, 66" x 78" and 84" x 96" (double size). Refer to the requirements tables for fabric and cutting. The main block construction is presented here. Refer to the *Flying Geese* construction section as necessary.

~ ~ ~ ~ ~ ~

These tables provide the requirements for constructing the 66" x 78" quilt top. It consists of 120 -6" blocks in a 10 block x 12 block setting, with a flying geese border. **CUTTING TIP:** If you lay the fabric #2 strip right sides together with the fabric #3 strip and again with the fabric #4 strip, before cutting with Companion Angle™, they will be ready for chain sewing. **SEWING TIP:** Always stitch these pairs together with the light fabric on top!

| Cutting Directions – 66" x 78" | | | |
|---|---|---|---|
| From | Cut | | To Get |
| Fabric #1 | 14 | 4¾" strips | 120 squares |
| | 7 | 2" strips | 184 Easy Angle™ triangles[1] |
| Fabric #2 | 29 | 2" strips | 480 Companion Angle™ triangles |
| | 7 | 2" strips | 184 Easy Angle™ triangles[1] |
| Fabric #3 | 14 | 2" strips | 240 Companion Angle™ triangles |
| | 11 | 2" strips | 184 Companion Angle™ triangles[1] |
| Fabric #4 | 14 | 2" strips | 240 Companion Angle™ triangles |

| Fabric Requirements | | |
|---|---|---|
| Fabric #1 | ▨ | 2¼ yards |
| Fabric #2 | ☐ | 2¼ yards* |
| Fabric #3 | ▨ | 1½ yards |
| Fabric #4 | ■ | 1 yard |

*Add 1 yard for double bias binding

[1]For the Borders

After cutting the fabric #2 (light) and fabric #3 and #4 (dark) Companion Angle™ triangles, stitch together using a ¼" seam allowance. Chain sew these pairs right sides together with the fabric #2 triangles always on the top, as shown to the right. Press the seams toward the darker fabric.

Attach the triangle pairs containing fabric #4 to opposite sides of the fabric #1 squares. Press the seams toward the square.

Add the triangle pairs containing fabric #3 to the alternate sides of the square. Press towards the square, then trim the "dog-ears." As simple as that, you have your blocks.

For the flying geese borders, construct the geese as shown earlier in the *Flying Geese* construction section, using fabric #1, #2, and #3. You will need 40 geese each for the top and bottom and 52 geese each for the sides. Add the side borders first, then the top and bottom borders.

After completing to this point, layer and quilt as desired. Hand baste ⅛" in from the edge of the quilt, then bind in fabric #2 with single 1¼" straight-of-grain binding, or a double bias binding.

The cutting chart below gives the requirements for the 84" x 96" (double) quilt top. You will make 195 -6" blocks and place them in a 13 x 15 block setting. The border requires 52 geese each for the top and bottom and 64 geese each for the sides.

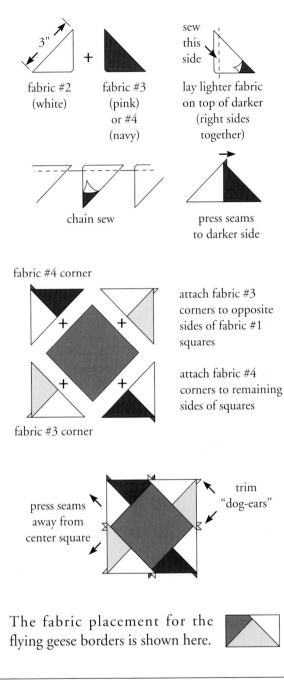

fabric #2 (white) + fabric #3 (pink) or #4 (navy)

sew this side

lay lighter fabric on top of darker (right sides together)

chain sew

press seams to darker side

fabric #4 corner

attach fabric #3 corners to opposite sides of fabric #1 squares

attach fabric #4 corners to remaining sides of squares

fabric #3 corner

press seams away from center square

trim "dog-ears"

The fabric placement for the flying geese borders is shown here.

| Fabric Requirements | | |
|---|---|---|
| Fabric #1 | | 3¾ yards |
| Fabric #2 | | 3¼ yards* |
| Fabric #3 | | 2¼ yards |
| Fabric #4 | | 1½ yard |

\* Add 1¼ yard for double bias binding

[1]For the Borders

| Cutting Directions – 84" x 96" | | | |
|---|---|---|---|
| From | Cut | | To Get |
| Fabric #1 | 22 | 4¾" strips | 195 squares |
| | 8 | 2" strips | 232 Easy Angle™ triangles[1] |
| Fabric #2 | 46 | 2" strips | 780 Companion Angle™ triangles |
| | 8 | 2" strips | 232 Easy Angle™ triangles[1] |
| Fabric #3 | 23 | 2" strips | 390 Companion Angle™ triangles |
| | 15 | 2" strips | 232 Companion Angle™ triangles[1] |
| Fabric #4 | 23 | 2" strips | 390 Companion Angle™ triangles |

# *Winter in the North Woods*

## *36" x 52"*

Would you believe this quilt was made without using any templates? Well, it was! Wouldn't it be wonderful to spend a long winter quilting while tucked away in a cozy cabin far from the rat race? That is, if one is provided with unlimited quilting supplies and lots of quilting friends nearby.

I've given directions for the quilt as shown, but since the mountains, trees, cabin, and stars are all done in block form, you may want to consider making some changes of your own. For example, you could appliqué other blocks or rearrange the motifs to personalize your quilt.

The entire white background on this quilt was stippled by machine, and the various motifs were then hand quilted. A small gold button was added for a doorknob and lace was put in the window.

*See photo on page 34.*

The graphic below shows the overall breakdown of the quilt. Any unspecified areas are background fabric. Design sections give the construction techniques for each type of block contained in the quilt.

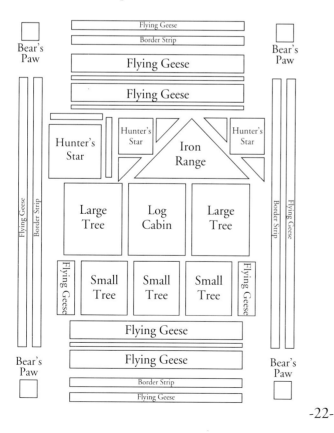

**The Log Cabin** – Assemble the door and window strips first. Following the cutting chart and the diagram, piece the bottom half of the cabin.

Add the triangles of the house to the roof piece. Add the two background triangles. Put the two halves of your cabin together.

Add background strips to the chimney. Center the chimney on the roof and sew seam. Trim off the excess of the background strips. Add the top and bottom strips.

**Flying Geese** – Use all the colors in your quilt and add scraps or purchase ⅛ yard pieces to have more variety. Refer to the *Flying Geese Construction* section for piecing your geese. Arrange your geese, twenty to a row, according to the diagram. Background strips are cut 1¼ " and are added between the geese and stars and between the rows of geese.

-22-

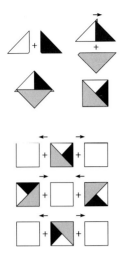

**Hunter's Star** – Add the background triangles to the dark brown triangles. (All units are the same, only turned.) Press seams toward the darkest fabric. Add these to the large gold triangles. Press in the direction of the arrow. Now assemble the star. Add the large background triangles to the small stars, then add to the sides of Iron

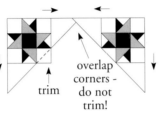

Range. Add 1½" strips (or the size needed) to two sides of the large star and mountain strips will measure 10½" x 30½".

**The Iron Range** – Chain sew all the triangle pairs. Sew together and press in the direction of the arrows. Piece the mountains.

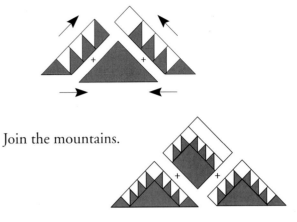

Join the mountains.

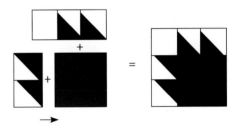

**Bear's Paw Corners** – Chain sew the triangle pairs. Press towards the black. Assemble the block as shown and press in the directions of the arrow.

**Trees** – Starting at the top of the tree, add the largest background trapezoids to the smallest tree trapezoids. Working down the tree, add the smallest background trapezoids to the largest tree trapezoids. Press seams towards the tree.

Match centers of each green trapezoid and piece trees from the top down. Notice the smaller trees eliminate two of the trapezoids. You will need to trim your tree blocks to size. Also notice the tree does not need to be centered in the block. This will allow more flexibility in placement.

Trim the small tree to 8" x 9¼" long. Trim the outside trees to 8¾" x 9¼" long. This row of three trees must equal 24½" x 9¼".

**Borders** – Add the geese strips to the top and bottom of the quilt, having the background triangles next to the block. Press towards the geese.

Next, add geese borders to the sides of the quilt. Place a Bear's Paw block at each end of the geese strips, referring to the diagram for placement. Now add the final borders.

You will need a variety of fifty geese for the outside border of your quilt. Cut and piece the geese as before. Piece the borders placing ten geese at the top and at the bottom and fifteen geese on each side, using the triangles cut with Easy Angle™ for the beginning and ends of your rows. NOTE: Know where your seam allowances will cross. These must be sewn exactly or your points will be cut off and the borders will be too long.

| Winter in the North Woods Cutting Directions (1) | | | | |
|---|---|---|---|---|
| Section | From | Cut | | To Get |
| Trees | Green | 4 | 2" strips | Companion Angle™ trapezoids: 5 -3", 2 -4", 5 -5", 5 -5½", 5 -6", 5 -7", 2 -8"[1,2] |
| | Background | 11 | 2" strips | Companion Angle™ trapezoids: 10 -5", 8 -6", 20 -7", 20 -8" Trunk strips: 10 -2" x 5" rectangles |
| | Med Brown | 1 | 2" strip | 5 -2" squares |
| Iron Range | Grey | 1 | 3¾" strip | 2 Companion Angle™ triangles 1 -3½" x 5" rectangle |
| | | 1 | 2" strip | 20 Easy Angle™ triangles[3] |
| | Background | 2 | 2" strip | 17 Easy Angle™ triangles[3] 3 -2" squares 1 -2" x 6½" strip |
| Hunter's Star | Dark Brown | 1 | 2½" strip | 2 -2½" squares |
| | | 1 | 3½" strip | 1 -3½" squares [4] |
| | | 1 | 2" strip | 4 Companion Angle™ triangles [4] |
| | | 1 | 1½" strip | 8 Companion Angle™ triangles |
| | Background | 1 | 2½" strip | 8 -2½" squares |
| | | 1 | 3½" strip | 4 -3½" squares [4] |
| | | 1 | 2" strip | 4 Companion Angle™ triangles [4] |
| | | 1 | 1½" strip | 8 Companion Angle™ triangles |
| | | 1 | 4½" strip | 4 -4½" Easy Angle™ triangles [5] |
| | | 1 | 1½" strips | spacing strips top/right of large star [6] |
| | Gold | 1 | 3½" strips | 4 Easy Angle™ triangles [4] |
| | | 1 | 2½" strips | 8 Easy Angle™ triangles |

Specific fabrics mentioned in the cutting chart are used only as a reference for construction and reference to the quilt on page 34. Feel free to choose your own colors.

[1] Don't cut 4" and 8" trapezoids for small trees.

[2] Finished base given (see page 10.)

[3] Cut 17 pair right sides together for triangle-squares.

[4] These pieces are for the 9" Hunter's Star.

[5] Add to the small Hunter's Stars to go around the Iron Range.

[6] Adjust strip width as needed to make Iron Range/Hunter's Star strip 10½" x 30½".

## Winter in the North Woods Cutting Directions (2)

| Section | From | Cut | | To Get |
|---------|------|-----|-----|--------|
| Log Cabin | Med Brown | Various Pieces | | 1 each of rectangles (front): 2" x 4½", 2" x 1½", 1½" x 4½", 1¾" x 2½", 1¼" x 1¾", 1" x 4½", 4½" x 4½" |
| | Dark Brown | 1 | diamond | largest Easy Eight™ diamond (roof) |
| | Gold | 1 | 3⅜" strip | 1 Companion Angle™ triangle (top) |
| | | 1 | 1¾" strip | 1 -1¾" square (window)[1] |
| | Red | 1 | 2" strip | 1 -3½" x 2" rectangle (door)[2] |
| | | | | 1 -1½" x 2" square (chimney) |
| | Background | 1 | 3¼" strip | 2 Easy Angle™ triangles |
| | | 1 | 1½" strip | 2 -5" strips (next to chimney) |
| | | | | 1 -10½" strip (below cabin) |
| | | 1 | 3½" strip | 1 -10½" strip (above cabin) |
| Bear's Paw | Red | 1 | 2½" strip | 4 squares |
| | Black | 1 | 1½" strip | 16 Easy Angle™ triangles[3] |
| | Background | 1 | 1½" strip | 16 Easy Angle™ triangles[3] |
| | | | | 4 -1½" squares |
| Geese | Various | Various | 2" strips | 92 Companion Angle™ triangles[4] |
| | Background | 7 | 2" strips | 184 Easy Angle™ triangles |
| | | 3 | 1¼" strips | spacing strips below flying geese rows[5] |
| Borders | Various | Various | 2" strips | 50 Companion Angle™ triangles[6] |
| | Background | 3 | 2" strip | 46 Companion Angle™ triangles[6] |
| | | | | 8 Easy Angle™ triangles |
| | Black | 4 | 2" strip | 2 -30½" strips for top/bottom |
| | | | | 2 -45½" strips for sides |

[1] Optional lace around window

[2] Optional button for doorknob

[3] Cut together for triangle-squares

[4] Cut Companion Angle™ triangles from several layers of 2" strips to save time.

[5] Adjust strip width as needed

[6] Cut Companion Angle™ triangles from several layers of 2" strips to save time.

### Fabric Requirements

| | | |
|---|---|---|
| Background | | 2 yards |
| Green | | ⅓ yard |
| Med Brown | | ¼ yard |
| Dark brown | | ¼ yard |
| Gold | | ¼ yard |
| Red | | ¼ yard |
| Grey | | ¼ yard |
| Black | | 1½ yards |

# Arizona Sunset
## 36" x 50"

*See photo on page 34.*

∿ ∿

*Arizona Sunset* was designed with a Southwest look in mind. Choosing different colors (Amish, for example) would give it an entirely different look. It is constructed in rows rather than blocks, so you could rearrange the strips or change them to suit your color scheme.

This quilt was hand quilted with lots of parallel lines following the shapes, giving the quilt an Art-Deco look.

NOTE: Maintain ¼" seam allowances throughout. Know where your seam allowances should intersect, or some of your points will be cut off and your strip will be too long. Each strip needs to measure 36½" in length. You will be constructing two of each strip, as they are repeated.

**Row 1** – Using the cut strips of peach and lavender that you have cut into the appropriate triangles designated in the cutting chart, assemble strips 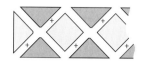 as shown here at the top, then join these into parallelograms.

**Row 2** – Now take the cut strips of green and peach that you have cut into the appropriate triangles, assemble as shown below, then press towards the darkest fabric.

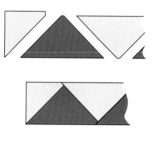

You are now ready to construct the flying geese units. Cut and assemble the geese from lavender, off-white, peach, and green.

**Row 3** – After you have completed the flying geese, assemble two rows consisting of a peach-green-lavender repeat. Both strips are the same, but one row is turned so the geese fly in opposite directions.

**Row 4** – You are now ready to construct the following:

Sew two rows of white and lavender trapezoids together; press towards the lavender.

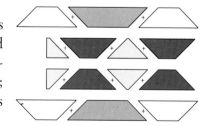

Sew the two rows together, matching and pinning at the seams. Add the two rows of off-white and lavender trapezoids, centering the lavender trapezoids. Trim excess fabric from the ends of these rows.

Now that the individual rows of this quilt are made, they will be put together from the center row out. Take the two cut strips of peach and sew to the top and bottom of the center strip. Add rows of flying geese to the top and bottom of this row, reversing the direction of one row of geese. Next add the rows of green to the top and bottom of your quilt. Then add the peach and green triangle rows, positioning your peach triangles next to the green strip. Now add the strips of off-white to the top and bottom, and finally add the lavender and peach rows, top and bottom.

Quilt as desired. Bind in lavender with straight-of-grain binding.

| Arizona Sunset Cutting Directions | | | | |
|---|---|---|---|---|
| Rows | From | Cut | | To Get |
| 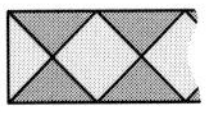 | Lavender | 3 | 2½" strips | 36 Companion Angle™ triangles |
| | Peach | 2 | 3⅜" strips | 16 -3⅜" squares |
| | | 1 | 2½" strip | 4 Companion Angle™ triangles |
| 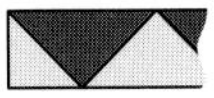 | Green | 2 | 3½" strips | 12 Companion Angle™ triangles |
| | Peach | 2 | 3½" strips | 4 Easy Angle™ triangles |
| | | | | 10 Companion Angle™ triangles |
| 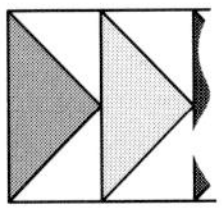 | Lavender | 1 | 4½" strip | 6 Companion Angle™ triangles |
| | Off-white | 3 | 4½" strips | 36 Easy Angle™ triangles |
| | Green | 1 | 4½" strip | 6 Companion Angle™ triangles |
| | Peach | 1 | 4½" strip | 6 Companion Angle™ triangles |
| 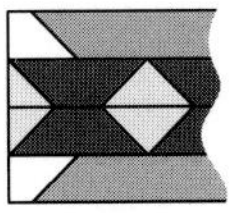 | Lavender | 1 | 2½" strip | 6 -9½" Companion Angle™ trapezoids[1] |
| | Off-White | 1 | 2½" strip | 8 -6½" Companion Angle™ trapezoids[1] |
| | Green | 2 | 2½" strips | 12 -6" Companion Angle™ trapezoids[1] |
| | Peach | 1 | 2½" strips | 10 Companion Angle™ triangles |
| | | | | 4 Easy Angle™ triangles |
| Spacing Strips | Off-White | 2 | 2½" strip | 2 -36½" strips |
| | Green | 2 | 2½" strips | 2 -36½" strips |
| | Peach | 2 | 2½" strips | 2 -36½" strips |

[1] Finished base given (see page 10.)

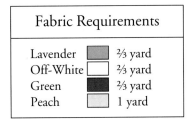

Fabric Requirements

| | | |
|---|---|---|
| Lavender | | ⅔ yard |
| Off-White | | ⅔ yard |
| Green | | ⅔ yard |
| Peach | | 1 yard |

Specific fabrics are mentioned in the cutting chart are only as a reference point to the photo pictured on page 34. Feel free to choose your own colors.

# Tree Of Life
## 53" x 73"

At last! A *Tree of Life* block done without the use of templates! This is a simple pattern, but the use of two colors gives the quilt a dramatic effect. Blue and white quilts such as this were quite popular in the 1800's.

In the past, women often used sewing scraps or the best parts of worn out clothing to piece their quilts. When they did have the luxury of buying new fabrics to make a quilt, they would often choose to make a two-color quilt. Indigo blue and white or turkey red and white were popular choices.

You may enjoy reviving this old tradition of two-color quilts. It does simplify the choosing and cutting of the fabrics!

*See photo on page 37.*

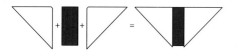

Begin by chain sewing all the triangle pairs together. Press towards the darkest fabric. Next, assemble the trunk. Sew the background triangles to each side of the trunk, then press towards the trunk.

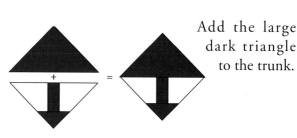

Add the large dark triangle to the trunk.

Take the twelve extra 2½" dark triangles and, with your Easy Angle™, trim off the second point of the other triangle. Position the triangles and sew the seam. Now trim the excess fabric below the seam.

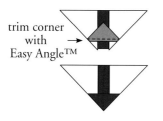

trim corner with Easy Angle™ →

Assemble triangle pairs into two rows of three and attach the rows to each other. Press all seams in a row in the same direction and alternate the directions between the rows. Assemble the two strips of triangle-squares and background squares (as shown) in the same manner. Attach rows of triangle-squares to the block.

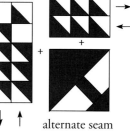

alternate seam directions by row

Proceed in this manner until you have completed twelve blocks. These will alternate on the diagonal with the six 10½" plain blocks. However, before you can assemble the blocks into a quilt you must cut the side triangle pieces. Take the three 15¼" squares cut from the dark fabric and divide each square into four triangles. These triangles will form the half-blocks that fill in around the sides of the quilt. Take the two 8" squares and cut on one diagonal to make the four corner triangles.

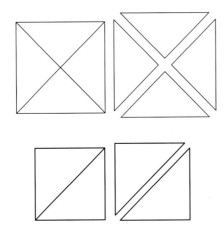

Starting in the upper left hand corner lay out the blocks and half-blocks into diagonal rows. The half-blocks and corner triangles have been cut to the exact size needed and no trimming should be necessary. Join the blocks and half-blocks in these diagonal rows then press towards the plain square or triangle.

NOTE: After the rows are stitched together and pressed, you *may* need to add fabric #2 strips to the sides of your quilt so that it measures 44½" wide. It will measure 56½" long, and you do not add any strips to the top and bottom. It is very important that the quilt measure 44½" x 56½" before adding the light borders strips.

Add the light border strips to the top and bottom of the quilt, then add the strips to the sides of the quilt. NOTE: *It is critical that your quilt measure 48½" x 60½" at this point for your sawtooth border to fit.*

**Sawtooth Border** – For this border you will use the 108 triangle pairs cut with Easy Angle™ and the 2½" squares cut from the background fabric for the corners of your strips.

Chain sew all of the triangle pairs, then press towards the darkest fabric. Trim the "dog-ears." For the top and bottom of the quilt, assemble in groups of twelve triangle-squares. For the sides of the quilt assemble in groups of fifteen triangle-squares. NOTE: Two strips of twelve (or fifteen) are joined so that the center triangle-squares are stitched together light fabric to light fabric, forming a mirror image.

sew mirror image sets of 12 and 15 triangle-squares
(2 sets of each number in each direction)

combine mirror image sets of 12 (do the same for 15)

Stitch the borders to the top and bottom of the quilt. Add the corner square to the ends of the side borders, then stitch these strips to each side of the quilt.

You will need to piece the strips for the outside borders to get the length you need. Stitch the outside border strips (cut 4¼") to the top and bottom of the quilt first, then add the side borders. Quilt as desired. Bind with double bias binding.

To construct the *Tree of Life* wallhanging (5" block), follow the directions for the larger quilt. Add a contrasting inner border cut at 1¼", then add an outer border cut at 3". Quilt as desired and bind with straight-of-grain binding.

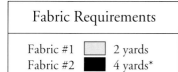
The fabric requirements to the left and cutting chart below are for the 53" x 73" quilt pictured on page 37.

| Cutting Directions – 10" Block | | | |
|---|---|---|---|
| **From** | **Cut** | | **To Get** |
| Fabric #1 | 3 | 3" strips | 24 Companion Angle™ triangles |
| | 13 | 2½" strips | 28 -2½" squares |
| | | | 276 Easy Angle™ triangles[1] |
| Fabric #2 | 2 | 4¾" strips | 12 Companion Angle™ triangles |
| | 2 | 1¾" strips | 12 -1¾" x 4" strips |
| | 12 | 2½" strips | 288 Easy Angle™ triangles[1,2] |
| | 6 | 10½" squares | 6 solid blocks |
| | 2 | 8" squares | 4 corner blocks |
| | 3 | 15¼" squares | 12 half-blocks |

[1]Cut together for chain sewing; includes 108 for the border
[2]Twelve extra for the base of the trunk

Wallhanging finishes at 21½" square – not quite small enough to be called a miniature!

| Cutting Directions – 5" Block | | | |
|---|---|---|---|
| **From** | **Cut** | | **To Get** |
| Fabric #1 | 2 | 1½" strips | 4 Easy Angle™ triangles |
| | | | 56 Easy Angle™ triangles |
| | 1 | 5½" strip | 1 -5½" center square |
| | | | 2 -5½" squares for corners |
| | 1 | 4½" strip | 4 Companion Angle™ triangles[1] |
| | 1 | 2⅝" strip | 4 Companion Angle™ triangles |
| | | | 4 -1¼" x 2½" rectangles (trunks) |
| Fabric #2 | 1 | 1¾" strip | 8 Companion Angle™ triangles |
| | 2 | 1½" strips | 56 Easy Angle™ triangles |
| | | | 8 -1½" squares |
| Fabric #3 | 4 | 1¼" strips | Inner borders |
| Fabric #4 | 4 | 3" strips | Outside borders |

[1] Cut for half-blocks.

# Spring Garden
## *47" x 47"*

*See photo on page 37.*

~ ~ ~ ~ ~ ~

*Spring Garden* is an adaptation of an old quilt block called "Turkey Tracks" or "Duck's Foot in the Mud." Done in lavender and green, this block now looks like a flower. The wallhanging could be made bed size by adding more large blocks in the center of the quilt and wider sashing and borders.

For *Spring Garden* you will piece forty-four flowers. (Refer to the section on sewing diamonds and setting in squares and triangles.) The piecing sequence for this flower is slightly different, and the steps are pictured here.

Start by setting in a background square between two diamonds (large floral) and a background square.

Add a background triangle and a lavender diamond to one side.

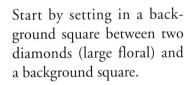

Then add a background triangle and a lavender diamond to the other side.

Finally add the corner triangle of fabric #2 (green).

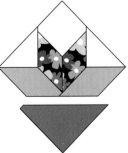

Four of these units are needed for each block, and four blocks are needed for the center of the quilt. A total of twenty-eight units are required for the border. Each flower block should measure 5½" square.

-31-

For the center blocks, set the flowers together with the background sashing and a center green square. Set the blocks together with four black sashing strips cut at 12½".

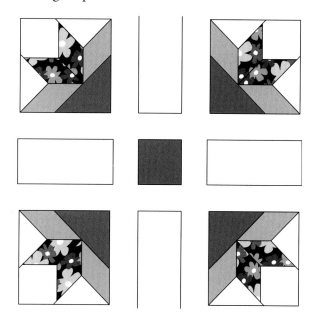

Strip piece the four inside borders in this sequence – 1" fabric #5 (black), 1½" fabric #2 (green), 2" fabric #3 (floral), and 1" fabric #2 (black). You may need to adjust the green and floral strip sizes so that the quilt measures 31½" square, raw edge to raw edge, at this point. Add these borders, mitering the corner. Refer to the section on mitering on page 70.

**Borders of Flowers** – Stitch three flower blocks together, so that the corner triangle point is at the bottom left of the block. Refer to page 31 graphic for placement. Make four of these units. Now stitch three flower blocks together so that the corner triangle point is in the bottom right of the block. Make four of these units. Stitch one of each of these units together so that the center of the strip has two corner triangles touching. You are creating mirror images. Add a 1" x 5½" black strip to each end. Make four of these. Sew two flower strips to the sides of the quilt.

Stitch the remaining four flower blocks to the ends of the remaining two strips. Attach these two strips to the top and bottom of the quilt.

Strip piece the outside borders in the sequence of – 1" black, 1½" green, and 2" floral. Add these strips to the quilt, mitering the corners.

Quilt as desired and bind in black.

| Fabric Requirements | | |
|---|---|---|
| Fabric #1 | | 1 yard |
| Fabric #2 | | 1 yard |
| Fabric #3 | | 1 yard |
| Fabric #4 | | ½ yard |
| Fabric #5 | | ⅔ yard* |

*Includes straight-of-grain binding.

| Cutting Directions – 12½" Block | | | |
|---|---|---|---|
| From | Cut | | To Get |
| Fabric #1 | 5 | 2" Easy Eight™ strips | 88 Companion Angle™ triangles |
| | 3 | 2½" strips | 44 -2½" squares |
| | 4 | 2½" strips | 16 sashing strips |
| Fabrics #2 | 3 | 3½" strips | 44 Easy Angle™ triangles |
| | 1 | 2½" strip | 4 -2½" squares |
| | | | 1 -1" squares |
| | 9 | 1½" strips | Borders |
| Fabric #3 | 7 | 2" Easy Eight™ strips | 88 diamonds cut with Easy Eight™ |
| | 9 | 2" strips | for borders |
| Fabric #4 | 7 | 2" Easy Eight™ strips | 88 diamonds cut with Easy Eight™ |
| Fabric #5 | 15 | 1" strips | Sashing and borders |

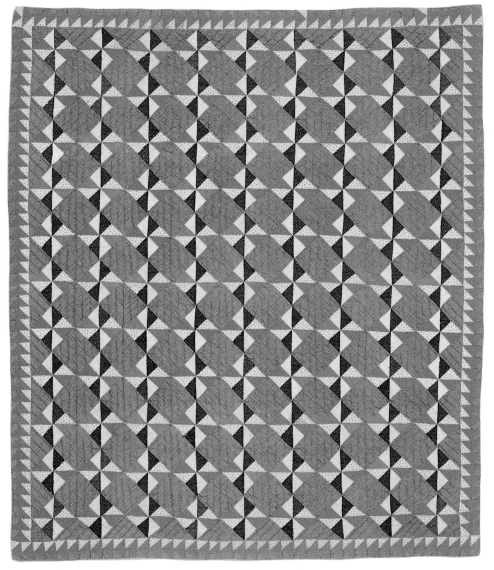

Antique *Right and Left, circa 1860*

66" x 76"
Even though this quilt was made
in the 1860's, I think it has a very
modern look to it.

Miniature *Right and Left*
is only 8½" square!

*Winter in the North Woods*

36" x 52"

*Arizona Sunset*

36" x 50"

*Winter in the North Woods*

Miniature
8¾" x 11"

*Arizona Sunset*

Miniature
8¾" x 11¼"

*Carpenter's Wheel*

67" x 85"

*Scrap Stars*

71" x 88"

*Tree of Life*

53" x 73"

*Tree of Life*

Miniatures – 11" square

*Spring Garden*
47" square

*Star Mosaic*

18½" x 30"

*Star and Frame*

23½" square

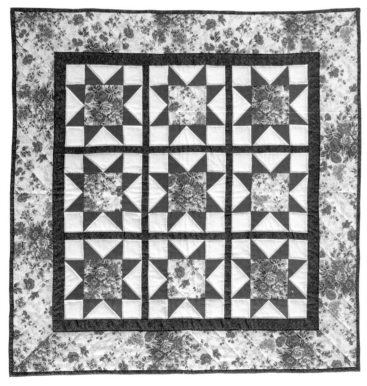

*Cranberry Stars*

26½" square

*Fourth of July*

9" x 11"

*Christmas Boxes and Bows*

40" square

*Wild Goose Chase*

51" square

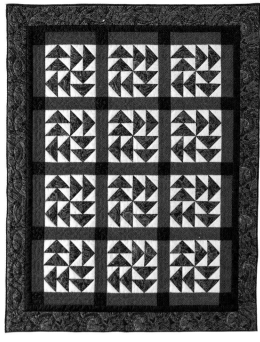

*Dutchman's Puzzle*

41" x 51½"

*Dutchman's Puzzle*

Miniatures
7¾" x 10¼"

*Amish Baskets*

35" x 41"

*Amish Baskets*

Miniature
12½" x 15"

*Amish*

Miniature
12" x 12"

# Star Mosaic

## 18½" x 30"

*See photo on page 38.*

≈ ≈

Suppose your border print looks like this.

Place the Easy Eight™ tool on an interesting segment of the pattern and cut several diamonds as close to the same design as possible. Repeat this for another interesting segment.

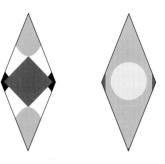

The segments you cut will be the diamonds used in the eight pointed star. Use only one design segment per star block.

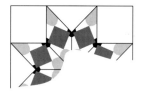

Refer to pages 14-15 in the tutorial section for setting in and piecing the eight pointed star.

Surprise! This entire quilt is constructed with only two fabrics – a border print and a background fabric. The stars are cut using Easy Eight™. Choose the size that fits the pattern best by looking through diamonds on the Easy Eight™ tool. Center part of the design in the diamond on the tool and cut. To change the star, center a different part of the design in the diamond and cut. A kaleidoscope pattern emerges as you sew the star together.

You will need to buy extra fabric as you will have more waste than usual. You may wish to buy one yard at first to experiment with, then purchase the necessary yardage for your project.

Add sashing between the star blocks, then add your borders. The finished size of your quilt will depend on which size diamond you cut.

No pattern or fabric requirements are given for this design, as border prints vary greatly.

# Dutchman's Puzzle
## *41" x 50½"*

*See photo on page 40.*

The *Dutchman's Puzzle* is a very versatile pattern. When made in strong, contrasting colors as pictured it makes a bold statement. It would also be a wonderful scrap pattern, using a variety of fabrics. Or, for another look altogether, use a striped fabric in the triangles. This would make the blocks look like they "spin."

Each *Dutchman's Puzzle* block consists of eight flying geese units, stitched together in groups of two, rotating each pair in a pinwheel configuration. The blocks will use the Companion Angle™ triangles together with the Easy Angle™ triangles. Size charts have been included for a wallhanging and a full size quilt. Refer to the *Flying Geese* section on page 16 for the directions on constructing the flying geese units.

Once you have completed the individual flying geese units, stitch all the units into groups of two as shown here. If you are making the smaller quilt shown above, you will need 96 units. If you are making the full size quilt you will need 160 units. You will make the flying geese units from fabric #1 and fabric #2. Press in the direction of the arrows.

Next, arrange these pairs into groups of two as shown below. It is important to rotate the groups in the direction shown. Press in the direction of the arrows.

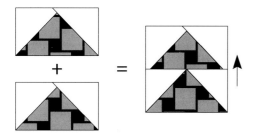

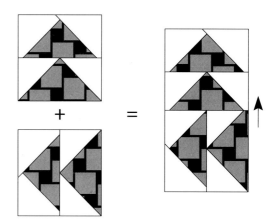

-42-

Finally, sew these pairs together as shown here to complete the blocks. You may want to pin at the seam intersections to prevent shifting. Press in the direction of the arrows. If you are making the smaller quilt, the blocks should measure 8½" at this point. If you are making the full size quilt your blocks should measure 12½" at this point.

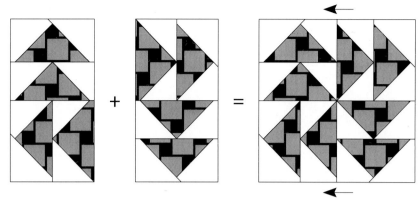

Cut your sashing strips from the width of your fabric (if you are making the smaller version), then cut into 31" pieces. A graphic is shown to the right. If you are making the larger quilt, you will cut 12½" strips and then counter-cut into your sashing strips.

You are now ready to assemble the quilt, using the blocks, the sashing strips, and the corner squares. Assemble into rows in the following sequence:

Row 1 – corner square-sashing-corner square-sashing-corner square-sashing-etc.
Row 2 – sashing-block-sashing-block-sashing-block-sashing-etc.

Continue in this manner repeating the Row 1-Row 2 sequence every other row ending with a Row 1 sequence.

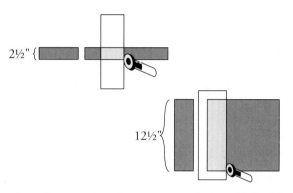

After the top has been assembled, add inside border strips of the accent fabric #4. Press the seams toward the outside. Next, add the outside borders of the large print, and press the seams toward the outside. Quilt as desired and bind with the accent fabric.

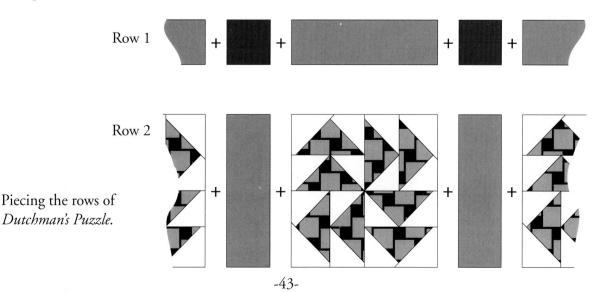

Row 1

Row 2

Piecing the rows of *Dutchman's Puzzle.*

| Cutting Directions – 8" Block (41" x 50½") | | |
|---|---|---|
| From | Cut | To Get |
| Fabric #1 | 8    2½" strips | 192 Easy Angle™ triangles |
| Fabric #2 | 8    2½" strips<br>5    3½" strips | 96 Companion Angle™ triangles<br>Outside borders |
| Fabric #3 | 6    2½" strips | 31 -2½" x 8½" strips |
| Fabric #4 | 2    2½" strips<br>5    1½" strips | 20 -2½" squares<br>Inside borders |

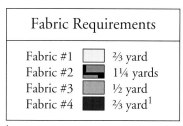

| Fabric Requirements | | |
|---|---|---|
| Fabric #1 | | ⅔ yard |
| Fabric #2 | | 1¼ yards |
| Fabric #3 | | ½ yard |
| Fabric #4 | | ⅔ yard[1] |

[1] includes straight-of-grain binding

*Dutchman's Puzzle*
*fabric and cutting charts*

| Fabric Requirements | | |
|---|---|---|
| Fabric #1 | | 1⅔ yards |
| Fabric #2 | | 3¼ yards |
| Fabric #3 | | 1½ yards |
| Fabric #4 | | 1 yard[1] |

[1] Add 1 yard for double bias binding.

| Cutting Directions – 12" Block (78" x 90") | | |
|---|---|---|
| From | Cut | To Get |
| Fabric #1 | 16    3½" strips | 320 Easy Angle™ triangles |
| Fabric #2 | 18    3½" strips<br>8    6½" strips | 160 Companion Angle™ triangles<br>Outside borders |
| Fabric #3 | 4    12½" strips | 49 -3½"x 12½" strips |
| Fabric #4 | 3    3½" strips<br>8    2" strips | 30 -3½" squares<br>Inside borders |

# Christmas Boxes and Bows

*40" x 40"*

*See photo on page 40.*

~ ~ ~ ~ ~ ~

Sometimes husbands can be very helpful. When my husband first saw a quilt I had made from the pattern "Lady of the Lake," he saw boxes in the design. Intrigued with this idea, I redrafted the pattern and chose Christmas colors – red and green plaids. *Christmas Boxes and Bows* is the result. The quilt contains many boxes or presents all neatly tied up with ribbon bows in the border.

There are many different ways to put this quilt together. When you have all your geese units assembled, invite your family and friends to help you arrange the blocks to your satisfaction. Assemble 64 flying geese units (see page 16) using fabric #2 (red) with fabric #3

(background). Assemble another 62 units using fabric #1 (green) and fabric #3. These units will be part of the blocks that make up the quilt. You will also cut 16 red and 20 green Companion Angle™ triangles which will form the corners of the blocks.

The border requires 44 bow blocks. Make 20 bow blocks from fabric #1 and fabric #3, and 24 bow blocks from fabric #2 and fabric #3. CUTTING TIP: After you have cut all your geese units, lay your red or green strips for your border bows, right sides together, with the white strips and cut the triangles together. They will be ready to chain sew!

After piecing the flying geese units and arranging them to your satisfaction, you are ready to construct the blocks. The directions here reflect my arrangement of two different blocks. Piece three geese units together alternating red and green and having a single Companion Angle™ triangle (no background triangles added) at the top.

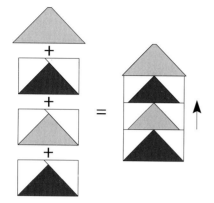

Next add the larger triangles cut with Companion Angle™ to either side of the geese strip. Make two sets for each block.

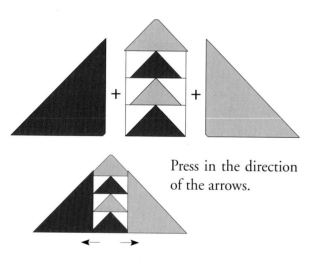

Press in the direction of the arrows.

The next step is to construct one cross piece for each block. Follow the graphic below and press in the direction of the arrows. There is a single triangle at each end of this strip.

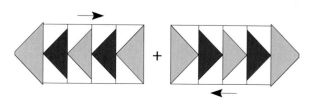

Finally, assemble the large blocks following the graphic. Pin at each seam intersection. Assemble all the blocks, alternating red and green.

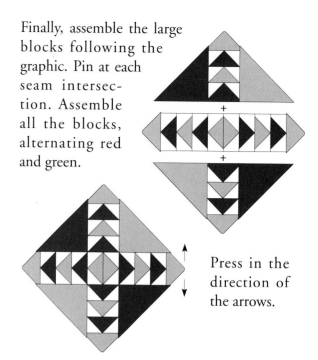

Press in the direction of the arrows.

Assemble the blocks into a 3 x 3 setting and add 1" green borders around the quilt. You may need to adjust the width so that your quilt measures 33" raw edge to raw edge at this point, so that your pieced borders fit properly.

Finished block with green in the corners. Make five blocks with green in the corners and four blocks with red in the corners.

**Borders** – Assemble all the units for the border following the graphic below, in the sequence of red-green-red-green-etc. Make four borders consisting of eleven bows. Seam on one of the short sides of the triangle, having the white triangle on top of the red or green triangle. See instructions in the *Right and Left* pattern for more information.

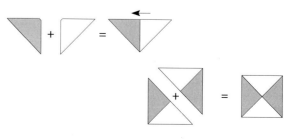

Attach top and bottom borders. Add green squares to the ends of the side borders, then add side borders to the quilt.

Quilt as desired. Bind in green with single 1¼" straight-of-grain binding.

These cutting and fabric charts are for the size pictured on page 39.

| Cutting Directions – 10½" Block | | | |
|---|---|---|---|
| From | Cut | | To Get |
| Fabric #1 (green) | 2 | 3¾" strips | 18 Companion Angle™ triangles[1] |
| | 8 | 2" strips | 82 Companion Angle™ triangles[2] |
| | | | 40 Companion Angle™ triangles[3] |
| | ½ | 3½" strip | 4 -3½" squares |
| | 4 | 1" strips | Inside borders |
| Fabric #2 (red) | 2 | 3¾" strips | 18 Companion Angle™ triangles[1] |
| | 8 | 2" strips | 82 Companion Angle™ triangles[2] |
| | | | 48 Companion Angle™ triangles[3] |
| Fabric #3 (background) | 9 | 2" strips | 252 Easy Angle™ triangles |
| | 6 | 2" strips | 88 Companion Angle™ triangles[3] |

[1] used for large triangles in blocks
[2] used for flying geese units in blocks
[3] used for bows in borders

| Fabric Requirements | | |
|---|---|---|
| Fabric #1 | ■ | 1¼ yards |
| Fabric #2 | ▨ | ¾ yard |
| Fabric #3 | □ | ¾ yard |

| Fabric Requirements | | | |
|---|---|---|---|
| | Twin | Full | Queen |
| Fabric #1 ■ | 2¾ yards | 3½ yards | 5 yards |
| Fabric #2 ▨ | 2½ yards | 3½ yards | 4½ yards |
| Fabric #3 □ | 2½ yards[1] | 3½ yards[1] | 4½ yards[1] |

[1] Add 1 yard for double bias binding.

| Cutting Directions for Larger Christmas Boxes – 14" Block | | | | | | | | | |
|---|---|---|---|---|---|---|---|---|---|
| From | Cut | | | | | To Get | | | |
| | Tw | Fu | Qu | | Tw | Fu | Qu | | |
| Fabric #1 (green) | 6 | 9 | 12 | 4¾" strips | 40 | 60 | 84 | | Companion Angle™ triangles[1] |
| | 14 | 21 | 30 | 2½" strips | 180 | 270 | 378 | | Companion Angle™ triangles[2] |
| | 6 | 7 | 8 | 2½" strips | 68 | 80 | 96 | | Companion Angle™ triangles[3] |
| | 1 | 1 | 1 | 4½" strip | 4 | 4 | 4 | | 4½" corner squares |
| | - | - | - | 2½" strips | - | - | - | | 2" finished side border |
| | - | - | - | 1½" strips | - | - | - | | 1" finished top/bottom borders |
| Fabric #2 (red) | 6 | 9 | 12 | 4¾" strips | 40 | 60 | 84 | | Companion Angle™ triangles[1] |
| | 14 | 21 | 30 | 2½" strips | 180 | 270 | 378 | | Companion Angle™ triangles[2] |
| | 6 | 7 | 8 | 2½" strips | 68 | 80 | 96 | | Companion Angle™ triangles[3] |
| Fabric #3 (background) | 22 | 33 | 46 | 2½" strips | 560 | 840 | 1176 | | Easy Angle™ triangles[2] |
| | 11 | 13 | 15 | 2½" strips | 136 | 160 | 192 | | Companion Angle™ triangles[3] |

Tw = twin size (68" x 80", 4 x 5 blocks)
Fu = full size (80" x 96", 5 x 6 blocks)
Qu = queen size (96" x 108", 6 x 7 blocks)

[1] used for large triangles in blocks
[2] used for flying geese units in blocks
[3] used for bows in borders

# Carpenter's Wheel

*67" x 85"*

*See photo on page 35.*

This pattern is also known by the name "Dutch Rose." The quilt pictured on page 35 was made in the late 1800's. It is a wonderful example of fine workmanship and exquisite quilting. Now you can duplicate this pattern using modern day tools! It's not a pattern for beginners, but anyone who has mastered setting in squares and triangles can attempt this quilt.

The first step in construction is to assemble the eight pointed stars in the center of each block. Complete directions are given on pages 14-15. After the center stars are complete, the rest of the block can be made. Follow the steps below and on the next page.

For the circle around the star, begin by piecing four units of dark-light-dark and four units of light-dark-light following the graphics below. The units must be pieced in this exact manner.

Join two pairs, adding set-in triangles. Repeat this procedure three more times. Once the pairs have been made, add them to the inside star, stitching to ¼" from the corner. Sew corner seams and set in the corner squares.

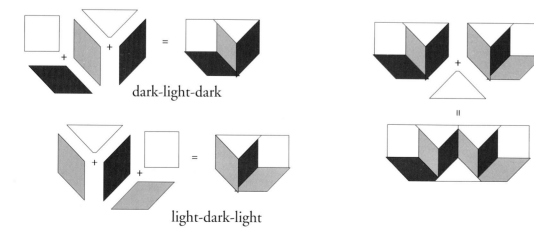

-48-

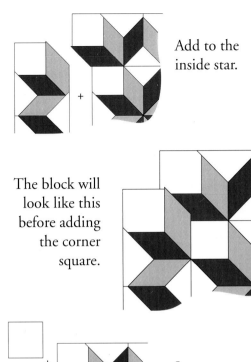

Add to the inside star.

The block will look like this before adding the corner square.

Sew corner seams and set in corner square.

Finished block.

After completing twelve blocks, set them on point, adding plain blocks (14" squares) between the pieced blocks, and half-blocks (from 21" squares) along the sides. Sew blocks together in diagonal rows. Include corner blocks cut from 14" squares. Refer to page 72 for more information on half-blocks.

Add three borders in the sequence fabric #1-fabric #2-fabric#3. Quilt as desired. Add double bias binding of the dark fabric.

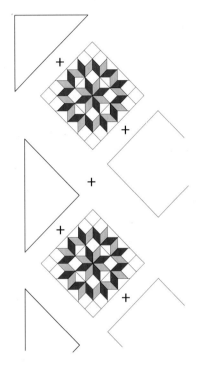

Diagonal set.

| Fabric Requirements | | |
|---|---|---|
| Fabric #1 | ■ | 1⅓ yard[1] |
| Fabric #2 | ▨ | 1⅓ yard |
| Fabric #3 | □ | 5¼ yards |

[1]Add 1 yard for bias binding.

| Cutting Directions – 13½" Block | | | |
|---|---|---|---|
| **From** | | **Cut** | **To Get** |
| Fabric #1 | 12 | 2" Easy Eight™ strips | 192 diamonds |
| | 8 | 2" strips | Borders |
| Fabric #2 | 12 | 2" Easy Eight™ strips | 192 diamonds |
| | 8 | 2" strips | Borders |
| Fabric #3 | 12 | 2½" strips | 192 -2½" squares |
| | 12 | 2" Easy Eight™ strips | 192 Companion Angle™ triangles |
| | 3 | 14" strips | 6 -14" squares |
| | | | 2 -14" squares |
| | 3 | 21" strips | 3 -21" squares |
| | 8 | 2" strips | Borders |

# Wild Goose Chase

## 51" x 51"

*See photo on page 39.*

F abric selection is very easy for *Wild Goose Chase.* I chose a very wild all-over print for the geese. It was interesting to see what happened to the pattern when it was cut up. Choose a neutral pattern for the background fabric and a dark, contrasting color for the solid bands. The high contrast between the colors gives the quilt a three-dimensional effect.

This is not a difficult pattern to piece, but ¼" seam accuracy must be maintained throughout if everything is to fit properly.

This quilt measure 51" square, but can be made larger or smaller by adding or deleting rows of geese and solid bands.

Obviously, this quilt consists of lots of flying geese units! Follow the directions found in the section about *Flying Geese* on page 16. Pay close attention to the cutting chart for the sizes of Easy Angle™ and Companion Angle™ triangles to cut. If the smallest geese size proves too difficult, substitute a solid band. Once you have completed all of the geese units follow the graphic illustrations for sewing together. NOTE: This quilt will be sewn together from the center out! The center block is constructed here, which in turn becomes the center of the next round, and so on until the top is completed.

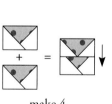

make 4

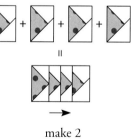

make 2

Chain sew the smallest geese together in pairs (above), and press. Add pairs to each side of the sashing square, and press. Add the geese strips to the center strip.

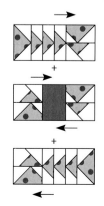

Add top and bottom 1½" border strips, then side border strips. Continue in this manner, alternating strips of geese and solid bands until the finished size is reached.

use as the center block
of next round of geese

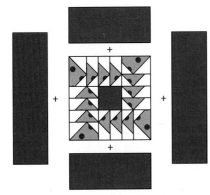

attach top and bottom first

| Fabric Requirements | | |
|---|---|---|
| Fabric #1 | ☐ | 1¼ yards |
| Fabric #2 | ▨ | 1¼ yards |
| Fabric #3 | ■ | 1½ yards[1] |

[1]Includes straight-of-grain binding.

| Cutting Directions | | |
|---|---|---|
| From | Cut | To Get |
| Fabric #1 | 6    3" strips | 128 Easy Angle™ triangles |
| | 4    2½" strips | 104 Easy Angle™ triangles |
| | 3    2" strips | 80 Easy Angle™ triangles |
| | 2    1½" strips | 56 Easy Angle™ triangles |
| | 1    1" strip | 32 Easy Angle™ triangles |
| Fabric #2 | 6    3" strips | 64 Companion Angle™ triangles |
| | 4    2½" strips | 52 Companion Angle™ triangles |
| | 3    2" strips | 40 Companion Angle™ triangles |
| | 2    1½" strips | 28 Companion Angle™ triangles |
| | 1    1" strip | 16 Companion Angle™ triangles |
| Fabric #3[1] | 1    1½" strip | 1 -1½" square |
| | | 2 -3½" x 1½" strips |
| | | 2 -5½" x 1½" strips |
| | 1    2" strip | 2 -9½" x 2" strips |
| | | 2 -12½" x 2" strips |
| | 2    2½" strips | 2 -18½" x 2½" strips |
| | | 2 -22½" x 2½" strips |
| | 4    3" strips | 2 -30½" x 3" strips |
| | | 2 -35½" x 3" strips |
| | 4    3½" strips | 2 -45½" x 3½" strips |
| | | 2 -51½" x 3½" strips |

[1] All solid border strips are cut the length of fabric.

# Amish Baskets

## *35" x 41"*

*See photo on page 40.*

Before starting your own Amish style quilt, you may wish to study pictures of Old Order Amish quilts to get a feel for their color choices.

You will need to choose several intense jewel tones and other fabrics with more subdued tones. The addition of black will make the colors sparkle.

This is a simple basket pattern that is set on point. The addition of the black triangles between the baskets is an unusual setting called "Streak of Lightning." I've quilted parallel lines in the zig-zag to further highlight this effect.

CUTTING TIP: Cut the colored triangles right sides together with black. They'll be ready to chain sew.

Chain sew all of the triangle-squares, then stack-press towards the black. Trim "dog-ears." Assemble the basket tops, making 12 sets of triangle-squares and 12 sets of triangle-squares with a square added to one end (see below). Press toward the black. Add these sets to the large triangle.

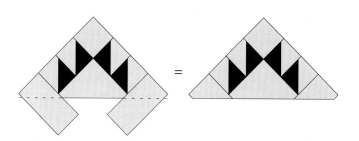

At this point, add rectangles to two of the basket blocks. They will be too big, so trim them even with the bottom of the large triangle. These are two of your half-blocks.

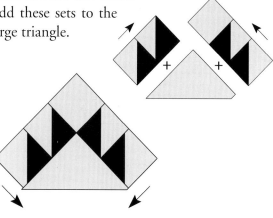

-52-

For the remaining ten baskets, add the bottom black triangles. Press.

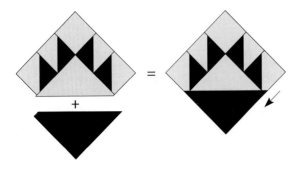

Add black triangles to background rectangles for the base of your basket. Make twelve of each. Press in the direction of the arrow. Add these to the baskets, then add the bottom triangle. Press in the direction of the arrow.

This is a finished basket block.

To assemble the remaining two half-blocks:

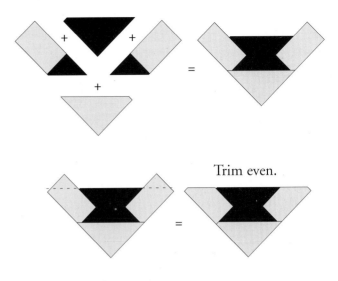

Trim even.

Now lay out the basket blocks in vertical rows on the diagonal. Sew the black side triangles to the basket blocks. Notice the two side rows begin with a basket bottom and end with a basket top.

Side rows.

Bottom of side row.

Center row.

The center row will use the smaller black triangles top and bottom.

Sew black triangles to the basket blocks.

After the strips are completed and have been pressed, you may need to trim. Carefully, leaving a ¼" seam allowance, trim from the point of each basket block.

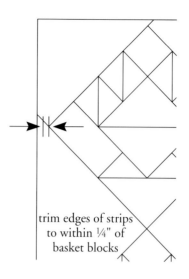

trim edges of strips
to within ¼" of
basket blocks

Join rows and add borders. Quilt in black and hand baste ⅛" from edge of quilt. Add straight-of-grain binding in the color of your choice.

| Fabric Requirements | | |
|---|---|---|
| Fabric #1 | ■ | ½ yard |
| Fabric #2 | ■ | ½ yard |
| Fabric #3 | ■ | ½ yard |
| Fabric #4 | ■ | ½ yard |
| Fabric #5 | ■ | ½ yard |
| Fabric #6 | ■ | 1½ yard |

| Cutting Directions – 6" Block | | | |
|---|---|---|---|
| From | Cut | | To Get |
| Fabrics #1, 2, 3 | 1 | 3½" strip | 4 Easy Angle™ triangles |
| | | | 4 -3½" x 2" rectangles |
| | 1 | 2" strip | 2 -2" squares |
| | | | 8 Easy Angle™ triangles |
| Fabrics #4, 5 | 1 | 3½" strip | 6 Easy Angle™ triangles |
| | | | 8 -3½" x 2" rectangles |
| | 1 | 2" strip | 3 -2" squares |
| | | | 12 Easy Angle™ triangle |
| Fabric #1 | 4 | 1½" strips | Inside borders |
| | 4 | 1¼" strips | Binding |
| Fabric #6 | 1 | 3½" strips | 12 Easy Angle™ triangles |
| | 4 | 2" strips | 24 Easy Angle™ triangles |
| | | | 48 Easy Angle™ triangles |
| | 4 | 5" strips | 22 Companion Angle™ triangles |
| | | | 4 Easy Angle II™ triangles |
| | 4 | 3½" strips | Outside borders |

# Cranberry Stars

## 27" x 27"

*See the photo on page 38.*

I fell in love with the floral print seen in the border of the quilt in the photograph on page 38. It was "the prettiest fabric in the whole world." And, of course, I didn't buy enough.

Using a floral print that doesn't have an even all-over design presents some challenges to the quiltmaker. After cutting several center squares the usual way, I discovered I was losing the design. I found I needed to center the square on the clumps of flowers. I also needed to be careful when cutting the borders to include some of the flower clumps.

Even though this quilt has a red and green color scheme, it looks like a traditional quilt rather than a Christmas quilt.

Refer to the *Flying Geese* section to make your star points. Fabric #2 (dark) is the star point. Assemble the star blocks following the graphic. Press in the direction of the arrows. Add sashing between the blocks and between the rows. Press toward the sashing. Join the inside and outside borders and press towards the outer border. Add these borders to the quilt and mitering the four corners.

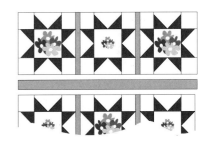

Quilt as desired and bind in straight-of-grain binding.

## Fabric Requirements

| Fabric #1 | 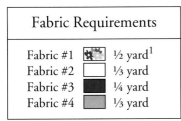 | ½ yard[1] |
| Fabric #2 | | ⅓ yard |
| Fabric #3 | | ¼ yard |
| Fabric #4 | | ⅓ yard |

[1] Need more for an uneven design.

| Cutting Directions – 6" Block | | | |
|---|---|---|---|
| From | Cut | | To Get |
| Fabric #1 | 5 | 3½" strips | 9 -3½" squares<br>4 Outside borders |
| Fabric #2 | 4 | 2" strips | 36 -2" squares<br>36 Companion Angle™ triangles |
| Fabric #3 | 3 | 2" strips | 72 Easy Angle™ triangles |
| Fabric #4 | 2 | 1" strips | 6 -6½" Sashing strips<br>2 -19½" Sashing strips |
| | 2 | 1½" strips | 4 Inside borders |
| | 3 | 1¼" strips | Binding |

# Star and Frame
### 31" x 31"

*See the photo on page 38.*

This is a quilt that is visually striking, but yet is fairly simple to make. Look carefully and you will see it is composed of nine blocks – five star blocks and four "art" blocks. I've selected a high contrast solid fabric for my frame, but perhaps you will want to try a border stripe to see what effect it will have.

Parallelograms are used in *Star and Frame,* and require a unique application of the Companion Angle™ tool. Detailed instructions are given below.

〜 〜 〜 〜 〜

Lay the two 3⅜" frame strips (fabric #4) right sides together. Place the Companion Angle™ with the bottom edge aligned with the top of your strips. Make your first cut.

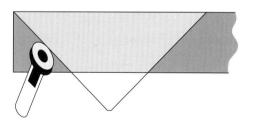

Now, on the very bottom edge of your strip, make a mark every 6½". Using the mark and Companion Angle™, cut your parallelograms.

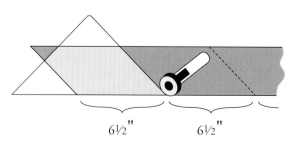

Assemble your dark and background triangles into one large tringle. Press in the direction of the arrow.

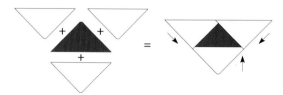

Set in the large pieced triangle. Refer to the *Setting In* section on page 14.

Assemble eight units of background and dark triangles. Press in the direction of the arrow. Add to the frame to complete the "art" block.

Refer to the *Flying Geese* section and assemble the star blocks as shown below. Press in the direction of the arrows.

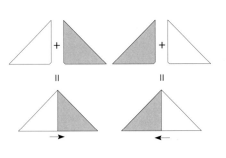

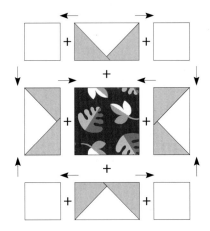

Assemble the blocks according to the layout on the previous page. Add the inside and outside borders either as a simple border or mitered border. Quilt as desired. Bind in straight-of-grain frame fabric.

| Fabric Requirements | | |
|---|---|---|
| Fabric #1 | | ⅔ yard |
| Fabric #2 | | ½ yard |
| Fabric #3 | | ⅓ yard |
| Fabric #4 | | ⅔ yard[1] |

[1]Includes border and straight-of-grain binding.

| Cutting Directions – 8" Block | | | |
|---|---|---|---|
| From | Cut | | To Get |
| Fabric #1 | 1 | 4½" strip | 5 -4½" squares |
| | 4 | 3½" strips | Outside borders |
| Fabric #2 | 5 | 2½" strip | 20 -2½" squares |
| | | | 40 Companion Angle™ triangles |
| Fabric #3 | 3 | 2½" strips | 40 Easy Angle™ triangles |
| | | | 8 Companion Angle™ triangles |
| Fabric #4 | 1 | 2½" strip | 4 Companion Angle™ triangles |
| | 2 | 3⅜" strips | 8 Parallelograms |
| | 4 | 1½" strips | Inside borders |

# Scrap Stars
## 88" x 88"

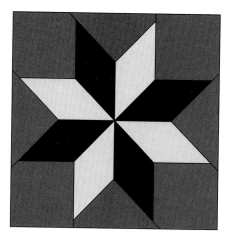

This 1930's quilt is done in a large variety of scraps. Instead of using muslin as the background behind the stars, as was typically done, it was used in the sashing strips. Also unusual is the edge finish of the quilt. The star blocks are set on point and sashing added. Then the quilt is simply bound, giving the quilt its lovely edge.

The star blocks in this quilt are quite small (5") and there are 142 of them. I've simplified the pattern by using the smallest size of Easy Eight™, which will give you approximately a 7" star block. This cuts the number of star blocks to 85. The quilt will now measure 88" square, a nice size for a double bed. You could add or subtract stars to change the size.

*See the phot on page 36.*

Piece all of the eight pointed stars, referring to pages 14-15. Notice in the graphic of the block, each star is composed of two different fabrics.

Lay out your stars in diagonal rows. Add the sashing strips between the stars and press toward the sashing. Assemble the sashing between the rows in the sequence of square-sashing-square. Press towards the squares. Join the rows. Quilt as desired and bind in double bias binding.

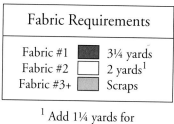

| Fabric Requirements | | |
|---|---|---|
| Fabric #1 | ■ | 3¼ yards |
| Fabric #2 | □ | 2 yards[1] |
| Fabric #3+ | ▨ | Scraps |

[1] Add 1¼ yards for double bias binding

| Cutting Directions – 7" Block (approx.) | | |
|---|---|---|
| From | Cut | To Get |
| Fabric #1 | 20   2½" strips <br> 11   2" Strips <br> 20   2" Easy Eight™ strips | 340 - 2½" Squares <br> 112 -2" Squares <br> 340 Companion Angle™ triangles |
| Fabric #2 | 9   7½" strips | 196 -2" x 7½" Sashing strips |
| Fabric #3+ | 1   2" Easy Eight™ strip <br> per fabric | 85 Stars with 2 fabrics / star |

# Miniatures

~ ~ ~ ~ ~

Both Companion Angle™ and Easy Angle™ are designed to help you make wonderful miniatures. Using the tools to cut your pieces has two benefits: Not only are your pieces more accurately cut, but you also save time in the cutting process.

I've used ¼" seams on all the miniature patterns. This lets you start with larger pieces, and ¼"seams are easier to sew and distort less than smaller seams.

Accuracy is the whole secret to making miniatures. You must be accurate in the cutting and sewing. As with most things, you will improve with practice.

You will find that once you adjust to the scale of miniatures, you will thoroughly enjoy making them. It's wonderful to be able to cut, sew, quilt and finish a quilt in one afternoon! This is also a chance for you to experiment with color combinations and patterns without investing large amounts of time and fabric.

After you've finished one of the larger projects in the book, I encourage you to try making the corresponding miniature.

## Tips on Working with Miniatures

- Sew accurate ¼" seams.

- Use only good quality 100% cotton fabrics.

- Use small prints or solids to keep everything in scale.

- Use a 70/11 new needle in your machine.

- Set your stitch length smaller.

- Choose high contrast fabrics.

- Never cut more than two layers of fabric at a time. More layers lead to inaccuracy in cutting.

- Pin at each seam intersection, but remove each pin as you come to it.

- Use "stack-pressing." It helps to hold the small pieces while pressing and keeps them from warping and stretching.

- Use only a dry iron until you have the entire quilt top finished. Then you may may want to use steam to square up your piece and set the seams.

- Avoid trimming blocks. Use borders to square up your quilt instead.

- Use a thin batting.

- Avoid seams wherever possible when quilting. Usually quilting in the ditch is enough for miniatures. Sometimes you may want to add some decorative quilting in the borders.

# Amish

## 9¾" x 10¼"

*See photo on page 40.*

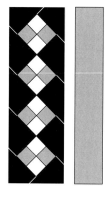

Add the Companion Angle™ triangles to these blocks, using Easy Angle™ triangles at the top and bottom of each row. Assemble into three rows. You may need to trim. See graphic on page 54 for trimming the blocks. Take the 1" bar strip and place between the rows, and also use as inside borders.

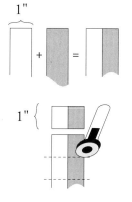

After cutting the 1" strips of each color, sew pairs of strips right sides. After sewing strips, cut apart into one inch segments. Reverse colors, and sew the pairs together. You will need to make twelve blocks.

Quilt in black. Add outside borders of black. Bind in black.

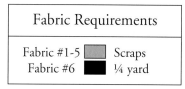

| Fabric Requirements | | |
|---|---|---|
| Fabric #1-5 | ▨ | Scraps |
| Fabric #6 | ■ | ¼ yard |

| Cutting Directions – 1" Blocks | | |
|---|---|---|
| From | Cut | To Get |
| Fabric #1-5 | 1    1" strip | 1" squares |
| Fabric #2 | 1    1" strip | 1" Bars between rows/inside borders |
| Fabric #6 | 1    1¼" strip | 18 Companion Angle™ triangles 12 Easy Angle™ triangles |
| | 1    2" strip | Borders |

# Amish Baskets

## 12½" x 15"

*See photo on page 40.*

~ ~

The graphics detailed below are the basket blocks and half-blocks that go into this miniature. As in the larger quilt, the baskets use various solid shades. CUTTING TIP: Lay your black strips right sides together with the basket strips and cut triangles together.

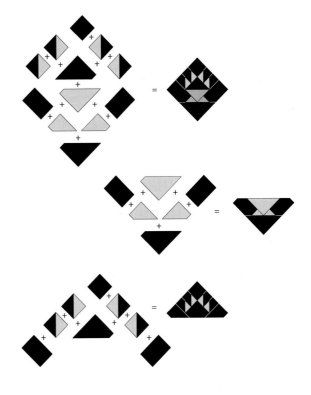

Notice the coloration in this quilt is reversed. Black was used as the background behind the baskets, then the baskets were placed in a "Streak of Lightning" set.

Assemble as you did for the larger quilt found on page 52. Quilt in black. Bind in straight-of-grain black binding.

### Fabric Requirements

| Fabric #1 | | Scraps |
|---|---|---|
| Fabric #2 | | Scraps |
| Fabric #3 | | Scraps |
| Fabric #4 | | Scraps |
| Fabric #5 | | ¼ yard |

| Cutting Directions – 2" Blocks | | | |
|---|---|---|---|
| From | Cut | | To Get |
| Fabric #1 | 2 | 1½" strips | 28 -1" x 1½" rectangles |
| | | | 24 Easy Angle™ triangles |
| | 2 | 1" strips | 12 -1" squares |
| | | | 48 Easy Angle™ triangles |
| | 1 | 1" strip | Inside borders |
| Fabrics #3, 4, 5 | 1 | 1½" strip | 2 Easy Angle™ triangles |
| | 1 | 1" strip | 12 Easy Angle™ triangles |
| Fabrics #2, 3 | 1 | 1½" strip | 3 Easy Angle™ triangles |
| | 2 | 1" strips | 18 Easy Angle™ triangles |
| Fabrics #5 | 4 | 2" strips | 22 Companion Angle™ triangles |
| | | | 4 Easy Angle™ triangles |
| | | | Outside borders |

# Right and Left
### *8½" x 8½"*

*See photo on page 33.*

≈ ≈ ≈ ≈ ≈ ≈

CUTTING TIP: Layer colors right sides together with the background strips and cut the triangle pairs from each color with the Companion Angle™ tool. The pieces of the block are detailed to the right.

Assemble as for the large quilt, except substitute 1¾" cut borders of your "square" fabric. Bind with straight-of-grain binding.

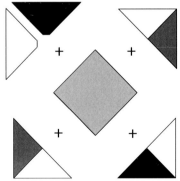

| Fabric Requirements | | |
|---|---|---|
| Fabric #1 | | ⅛ yard |
| Fabric #2 | | ⅛ yard |
| Fabric #3 | | ⅛ yard |
| Fabric #4 | | ⅛ yard |

| Cutting Directions – 2" Block | | |
|---|---|---|
| From | Cut | To Get |
| Fabric #1 | 1 1⅞" strip<br>1 1¾" strip | 9 -1⅞" squares<br>Borders |
| Fabric #2 | 1 1" strip | 36 Companion Angle™ triangles |
| Fabric #3 | 1 1" strip | 18 Companion Angle™ triangles |
| Fabric #4 | 1 1" strip | 18 Companion Angle™ triangles |

# Sailing, Sailing

*7¾" x 9"*

This is a charming miniature quilt using a simplified version of the traditional sailboat block. I've set the sailboat blocks together with plain blocks printed with an old sailing ship.

Add the background triangles to both sides of the red trapezoid.

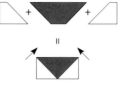

Assemble six triangle-squares from blue and background. Press. Assemble each sail section and prees in the direction of the arrows as shown.

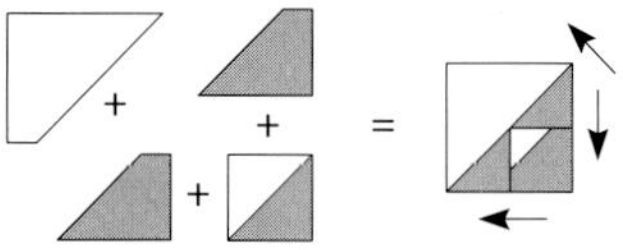

Now add the larger background rectangle. Press.

Add to the bottom of the boat. Press.

Join blocks in rows, alternating pieced blocks with printed blocks. Add inside and outside borders.

Quilt in the ditch between blocks and around the sailboat, if desired. Also quilt around inside border. Bind in red.

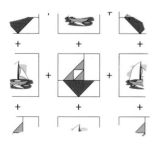

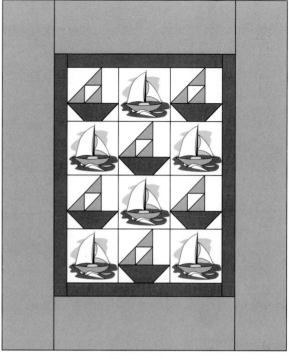

*No photo given.*

| Fabric Requirements | | |
|---|---|---|
| Fabric #1 | boat | ⅛ yard |
| Fabric #2 | | ⅛ yard |
| Fabric #3 | | ⅛ yard |
| Fabric #4 | | ⅛ yard |
| Fabric #5 | | ⅛ yard |

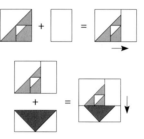

| Cutting Directions – 1½" Blocks | | | |
|---|---|---|---|
| From | Cut | | To Get |
| Fabric #1 | 6 | 2" squares | 6 Squares with Sailboates centered |
| Fabric #2 | 1 | 1" strip | 18 Easy Angle™ triangles |
| | 1 | 1½" strip | 6 Easy Angle™ triangles |
| | | | 6 -1" x 1½" rectangles |
| Fabric #3 | 1 | 1" strip | 6 Companion Angle™ 1½" trapezoids[1] |
| | 1 | ⅞" strip | Inside Border |
| | 1 | 1¼" strip | Binding |
| Fabric #4 | 1 | 1" squares | 18 Easy Angle™ triangles |
| Fabric #5 | 1 | 1½" strip | Outside Border |

[1] Finished base given (see page 10.)

-63-

# Dutchman's Puzzle

*7¾" x 10¼"*

*See photographs on page 40.*

As for the large *Dutchman's Puzzle*, each block in the miniature version has eight flying geese units. Refer to the *Flying Geese* construction section on page 16 for more information.

The basic block formation is shown below. Follow this procedure to construct six *Dutchman's Puzzle* blocks. Place sashing of the accent fabric between the blocks and place an inside border around the blocks. Outside borders are from fabric #3.

Quilt as desired. Bind in the accent fabric.

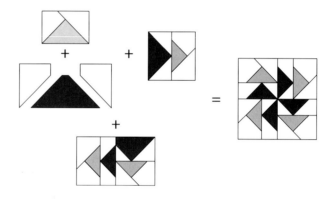

| Fabric Requirements | |
|---|---|
| Fabric #1 ☐ | Scraps |
| Fabric #2 ▨ | Scraps |
| Fabric #3 ▨ | Scraps |
| Fabric #4 ■ | Scraps |

| Cutting Directions – 2" Block | | |
|---|---|---|
| From | Cut | To Get |
| Fabric #1 | 2   1" strips | 96 Easy Angle™ triangles |
| Fabric #2 | 1   1" strip | 24 Companion Angle™ triangles |
| Fabric #3 | 1   1½" strip | Outside borders |
| Fabric #4 | 1   ⅞" strip | Sashing and inside borders. |

# Fourth of July
## *9" x 11"*

This miniature quilt uses a favorite block of mine – the Sawtooth Star. In each of the 1" center squares I've put a small flag. These flags were cut out of a printed fabric.

Add navy stars points to background triangles. Add to center square. Add corner squares to remaining units. Assemble the star as detailed in the graphic below.

Add sashing between blocks. Press towards sashing. Assemble two units that consist of sashing-square-sashing strips. Join rows. Add inside red borders and outside navy borders.

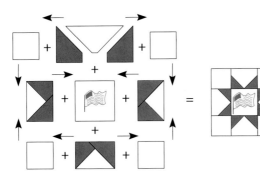

Quilt in the ditch around center square and inside each block. Quilt around inside border, and quilt a design in the border, if desired. Bind with red straight-of-grain binding.

### Fabric Requirements

| Fabric | | |
|---|---|---|
| Fabric #1 | flag | ⅛ yard |
| Fabric #2 | ▢ | ⅛ yard |
| Fabric #3 | ▢ | ⅛ yard |
| Fabric #4 | ▢ | ⅛ yard |

### Cutting Directions – 2" Blocks

| From | Cut | | To Get |
|---|---|---|---|
| Fabric #1 | 6 | 1½" squares | 6 -Flags centered in the square |
| Fabric #2 | 2 | 1" strips | 48 Easy Angle™ triangles<br>2 -⅞" squares |
| | 1 | 2" strip | Outside borders |
| Fabric #3 | 2 | 1" strips | 24 -1" squares<br>24 Companion Angle™ triangles |
| Fabric #4 | 2 | ⅞" strips | 7 -2½" x ⅞" Sashings<br>Inside borders |
| | 1 | 1¼" strip | Binding |

# Tree of Life
## 11" x 11"

Assemble the trees according to the directions given for the larger quilt found on page 28. TIP: Chain-sew wherever possible to avoid the tendency of the sewing machine to chew small pieces.

Assemble the quilt in diagonal rows. Press, and then trim to approximately 8" square, leaving ¼" seam allowances. Add borders of dark fabric to the quilt.

Do a minimum of quilting in the tree blocks. I generally quilt only in the ditch on the miniatures, avoiding the thick seam allowances whenever possible. The center and half-blocks are quilted in a half inch grid. A simple design is quilted in the border. Bind with straight-of-grain binding.

*See photos on page 37.*

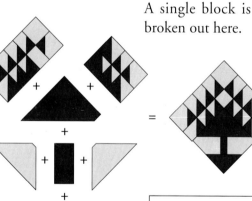

A single block is broken out here.

Refer to page 28 for base of block cutting and sewing.

| Fabric Requirements | | |
|---|---|---|
| Fabric #1 | ■ | ¼ yard[1] |
| Fabric #2 | ▫ | ¼ yard |
| Fabric #3 | ▨ | ¼ yard |

[1] Scraps if making a scrap quilt.

[1] Cut light and dark fabric together.

[2] See page 72

| Cutting Directions – 2½" Block | | | |
|---|---|---|---|
| From | Cut | | To Get |
| Fabric #1 | 1 | 2" strip | 4 Easy Angle™ triangles<br>4 -¾" x 1½" rectangles |
| | 2 | 1" strips | 56 Easy Angle™ triangles[1]<br>4 extra 1" triangles for base of tree |
| Fabric #2 | 2 | 1" strips | 56 Easy Angle™ triangles[1]<br>8 -1" squares |
| | 1 | 1⅛" strip | 8 Companion Angle™ triangles |
| Fabric #3 | 3 | 3"squares | 1 Center square<br>4 Corner triangles[2] |
| | 1 | 2¾" strip | 4 Companion Angle™ triangles |

# Arizona Sunset

## 8¾" x 11¾"

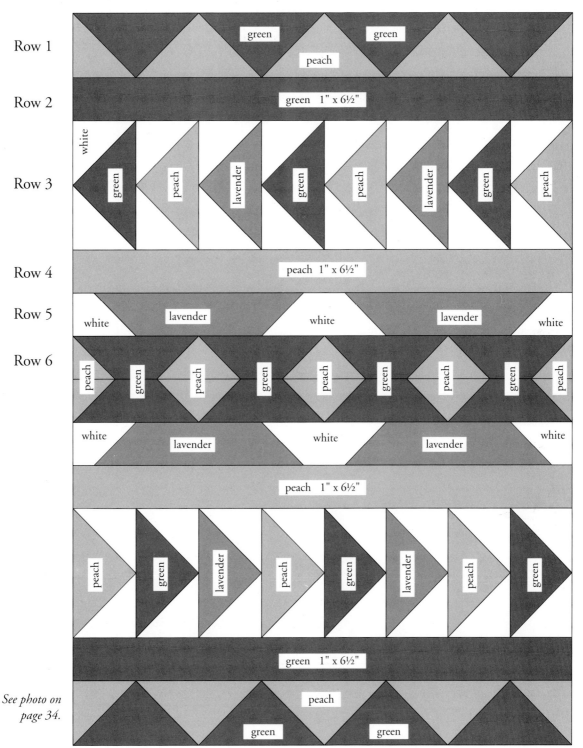

Row 1

Row 2

Row 3

Row 4

Row 5

Row 6

*See photo on page 34.*

For Rows 1 and 3, cut 1¼" strips for your Companion Angle™ and Easy Angle™ triangles. For Rows 5 and 6, cut 1" strips for your triangles and trapezoids. Cut the base of the small trapezoid on the 2" doted line and the large trapezoid on the 3" dotted line of Companion Angle™.

Follow piecing instructions given for the larger version of *Arizona Sunset*. Quilt as desired and bind in green fabric.

# Winter in the North Woods

*8¾" x 11"*

*See photo on page 34.*

Refer to each section (such as trees) of the larger quilt for specific instruction. The star in this miniature *Winter in the North Woods* is *not* the Hunter's Star, but a Friendship Star. Assembly and pressing directions are the same.

A piecing breakdown of this quilt is detailed below. Cutting and fabric charts are provided on the following page. The roof of the cabin requires a parallelogram. The Companion Angle™ instructions for this technique can be found on page 56.

Add a border and quilt as desired.

≈ ≈

Trees should be trimmed to 3" unfinished. All pieces are sized proportionately.

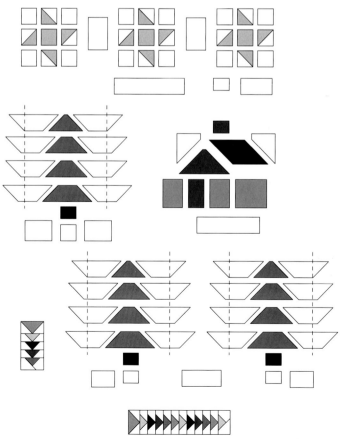

-68-

| Cutting Directions | | | |
|---|---|---|---|
| Section | From | Cut | To Get |
| Log Cabin | Dark Brown | 1   1½" strip | parallogram (2¼" long side) [1] |
| | Med Brown | 1   1¾" strip | 2 -1¾" x 1¼" strips (walls)<br>1 -1¾" x 2" strip (walls) |
| | Dark Red | 1   1½" strip | 1 Companion Angle™ triangle<br>1 -1¾" x1" rectangle (door)<br>1 -¾" x1" rectangle (chimney) |
| | Background | 1   1" strip | 1 - 1" x 4½" strip (above cabin)<br>1 - 1" x 2" strip (above cabin)<br>1 - 1" x 4" strip (below cabin)<br>1 -¾" x1" rectangle (above chimney) |
| | | 1   1½" strip | 2 Easy Angle™ triangles |
| Trees | Dark Green | 1   1" strip | 3 Companion Angle™ triangles<br>3 -2", 6 -1½" Companion Angle™ trapezoids [2] |
| | Dark Brown | 1   1" strip | 3 -1" x  ¾" strips (tree trunks) |
| | Background | 2   1" strips | 24 Companion Angle™ trapezoids [2]<br>2 -1" x  ¾" (below lower tree trunks)<br>2 -1¼" x 1½" strips (below top tree)<br>2 -1" x 1½", 1 -1" x 2½" rectangles [3]<br>1 -1" square (below single tree trunk) |
| Stars | Gold | 1   1" strip | 3 -1" squares<br>12 Easy Angle™ triangles [4] |
| | Background | 2   1" strips | 12 -1" squares<br>12 Easy Angle™ triangles [4] |
| | | 1   1¼" strip | 2 -1¼" x 2" strips (between stars) |
| Geese | Various | Various   1" strips | 17 Companion Angle™ triangles |
| | Background | 1   1" strip | 34 Easy Angle™ triangles |
| Borders | Dark Brown | 1   1½" strip | border |
| | Dark Red | 1   1¼" strip | binding |

[1] Use Companion Angle™ to cut from  a 1½"  x 4" strip
[2] Cut base at 2"
[3] Beside bottom tree trunks
[4] Cut gold and background triangles together

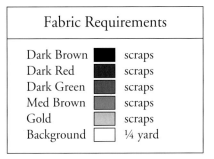

| Fabric Requirements | | |
|---|---|---|
| Dark Brown | | scraps |
| Dark Red | | scraps |
| Dark Green | | scraps |
| Med Brown | | scraps |
| Gold | | scraps |
| Background | | ¼ yard |

# Finishing the Projects

≈ ≈ ≈ ≈ ≈

## BORDERS

Almost every quilt has a border. Don't neglect this part of the quilt. Think of the border as a frame for your quilt. I prefer to use the same colors in the borders that I have used in the blocks. Generally, the darker fabrics look best in the border and/or binding.

Whether you put on simple borders, pieced borders or mitered borders, it's important to measure through the middle of your quilt in several places and take an average of these measurements. You may find the edges of the quilt have stretched somewhat through handling. The borders can help "square-up" your quilt. It is especially important on wall-hangings.to have borders that are even and ripple-free.

## MITERED CORNERS – MADE EASY WITH COMPANION ANGLE™

Step 1: Add borders to all four sides of your quilt, allowing several extra inches for the borders to extend beyond the edges of the quilt and overlapping each other. Stitch to within ¼" from the corner.

Step 2: Fold the quilt on the diagonal, right sides together, matching raw edges, and having the borders extending outward.

Step 3: Lay Companion Angle™ on your quilt with the longest edge on the diagonal fold and the side on the raw edges. You can mark your sewing line on the borders with a pencil, pin and sew the mitered seam. Check the right side before you trim off the excess fabric.

### OR

If you're comfortable with making mitered corners, you may wish to eliminate the marking and go on with Step 4.

Step 4: Extend Companion Angle™ ¼" beyond the fold. Align fold line with 10" dashed line. This will add a seam allowance to your borders. Cut along the edge of your tool.

Step 5: Pin and sew the mitered corner.

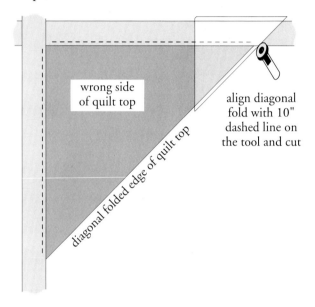

## PREPARING FOR QUILTING

When your quilt top is completed, give it a final pressing. Mark any quilting lines lightly. Be sure to test your marking pencil or tool on a scrap of fabric first. You should be able to remove the mark with a fabric eraser or mild soap and water.

Cut your batting and backing several inches larger than your quilt top. (A thin batt is best for wall quilts and miniatures.) Using masking tape, tape your backing, right side down to a clean flat surface, pulling it taut. Add your batting next, but do not tape it down. Add your quilt top, right side up, and tape this down as before. Now, hand baste in a 4" or smaller grid over the entire surface of the quilt top. Small safety pins may be used to pin-baste, pinning every few inches. When basting is completed, remove the tape. You're now ready to quilt.

## QUILTING

There's no mystery to the quilting stitch – it's merely a running stitch. Ideally the stitches should be straight, even, and tiny. Don't despair – your stitching will improve with practice! Use a small betweens needle and quilting thread. Off-white is a good choice for most quilts. All of your knots should be popped to the inside layer and hidden. You can quilt in your lap or use a hoop or frame of your choice. Generally, it's best to start in the center of your quilt and work towards the outside.

When you've finished quilting, hand baste ⅛" around the edge of the quilt. This will hold the three layers together and prevent the edge from stretching while you sew on the binding. Do not trim the excess batting and backing until after the binding is sewn in place.

## BIAS BINDING

A good choice for large quilts is a double bias binding. Allow one yard for binding. Cut strips on the bias 2½" wide, seaming pieces together. Press seams open. Fold binding in half, wrong sides together, and press, being careful not to stretch it. Lay folded binding on the right side of the quilt top, align raw edges, and stitch a ¼" seam. You may wish to leave some excess batting and backing to fill up the binding when you turn it to the back. Stitch the folded edge in place by hand, covering your stitching line on the back.

## BINDING

Lap size or smaller quilts generally need only a single, straight-of -grain binding. Seam together enough 1¼" wide strips to go around the entire outside edge of the quilt, allowing several extra inches for the corners and overlapping. Press

seams open, and press the beginning edge under at least ¼". Starting at the bottom edge of the quilt, sew on the binding using a ¼" seam. Stitch up to ¼" from the first corner, stop and backstitch. Remove the quilt from the machine. Fold the binding away from the quilt as shown, then fold again to place the binding along the next edge of the quilt. This fold creates an angled pleat at the corners when turned. Begin stitching at the edge. Repeat at each corner. To end, simply overlap the beginning fold by 1".

Trim away excess batting and backing. Turn binding under ¼" and blindstitch in place on the back, covering your stitching. Use matching thread and a fine, thin needle. Don't allow your stitches to go through the front of the quilt.

Sign and date your quilt.

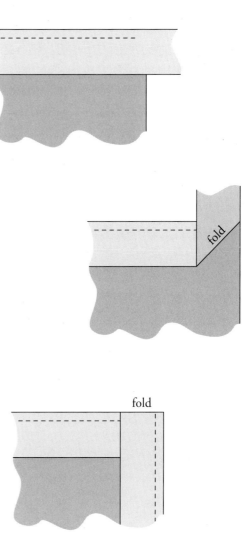

# Half-Blocks

Quilt blocks set on point need half-blocks to complete the sides. These triangles should have the longest side cut on the straight grain of the fabric. Companion Angle™ can cut these half-blocks for your wall quilts – up to a 7" finished block. Use the table provided here to determine which size triangle to cut. Some of these triangles will be sightly larger than you need. That's okay! Trim carefully after sewing.

To cut the corner triangles, cut two squares the same size as your finished block, then cut on the diagonal. These will also be a bit larger than needed. Once again, trim carefully after sewing.

For larger half-blocks, measure the unfinished block, add two seam allowances and multiply this total by 1.5. This should give adequately large half-blocks. Trim after sewing.

| Half-block Cutting Directions | | |
| --- | --- | --- |
| Finished Block Size | Strip Width to Cut | Finished Triangle Size |
| 2" block | 2" strip | 3" Companion Angle™ triangles |
| 2½" block | 2¼" strip | 3½" Companion Angle™ triangles |
| 3" block | 2¾" strip | 4½" Companion Angle™ triangles |
| 3½" block | 3" strip | 5" Companion Angle™ triangles |
| 4" block | 3½" strip | 6" Companion Angle™ triangles |
| 4½" block | 3¾" strip | 6½" Companion Angle™ triangles |
| 5" block | 4" strip | 7" Companion Angle™ triangles |
| 5½" block | 4½" strip | 8" Companion Angle™ triangles |
| 6" block | 4¾" strip | 8½" Companion Angle™ triangles |
| 6½" block | 5¼" strip | 9½" Companion Angle™ triangles |
| 7" block | 5½" strip | 10" Companion Angle™ triangles |

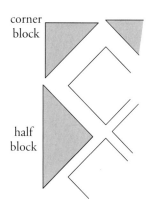

corner block

half block

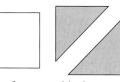

for corner blocks use finished block size and cut diagonally

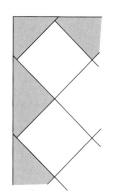

carefully trim after sewing leave seam allowance)

for larger half blocks cut large square on both diagonals